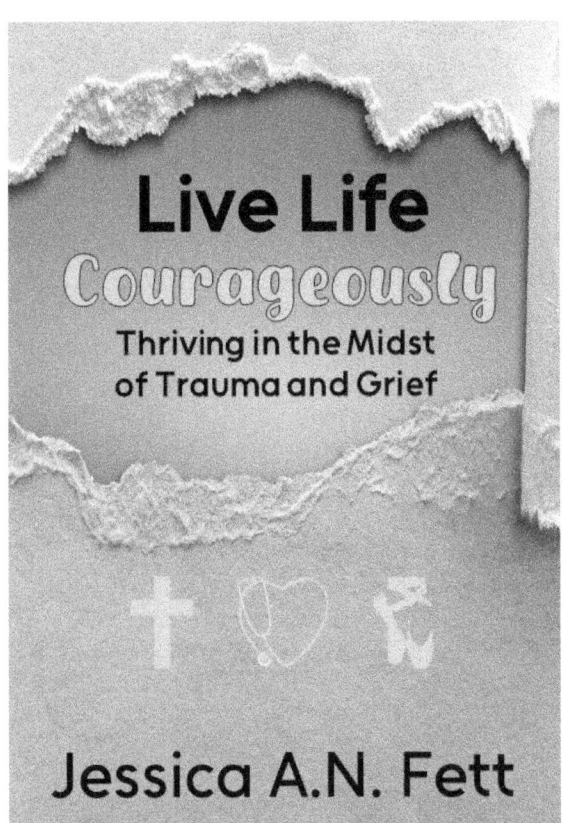

© 2025 Jessica A.N. Fett

Paperback ISBN-13: 979-8-9932396-0-6
Digital ISBN-13: 979-8-9932396-1-3

All rights reserved. No part of this publication may be reproduced or transmitted in any form or by any means without written permission from the publisher.

Scripture verses marked CSB are taken from The Christian Standard Bible, (CSB). Copyright © 2017 by Holman Bible Publishers. Used by permission. Christian Standard Bible®, and CSB® are federally registered trademarks of Holman Bible Publishers, all rights reserved.

Scripture verses marked NIV are taken from the Holy Bible, New International Version®, NIV®. Copyright © 1973, 1978, 1984, 2011 by Biblica, Inc.™ Used by permission of Zondervan. All rights reserved worldwide. www.zondervan.com.

Scripture verses marked ESV are taken from The ESV® Bible (The Holy Bible, English Standard Version®), © 2001 by Crossway, a publishing ministry of Good News Publishers. ESV Text Edition: 2025.

Published by Jessica A.N. Fett

Dedication

*To my father, Reginald E. Carveth II,
who taught me how to be courageous and nurturing.*

Author's Notes

Cherished Reader,

    I started this project with the intent to develop it as a companion book to an interactive journal that I compiled called "Nitty-Gritty Healthy 7 Week Challenge." The writing journey for this story revealed a different path as the pages awoke with the strokes of the keyboard. Key topics are developed as woven through my experiences. Scientific terms and theories will be touched on in the broader story. Words like fight, battle, struggle, and conflict have been used by many to characterize the difficulties and oppositions in life. I use these words cautiously in the following pages from the perspective of a survivor of health issues, violence, and adversity.

Kindling Courage

    You may have picked up this book out of pure curiosity. You may have chosen it because you are searching for help. Or, you may have selected it because there is a hole in your heart that you are desperate to fill. Whatever the reason, dear one, may you be blessed with the Words of God woven through these stories.

A **Kindling Courage** section is at the end of every chapter. This is for you to jot down notes and answer questions to help dig deeper into the Word. Use these opportunities to deepen your relationship with God and to understand your own thoughts better. Our thoughts either sustain life or destroy it; they can be used as weapons or as medicine.

Your sister in Christ,
Jessica A. N. Fett

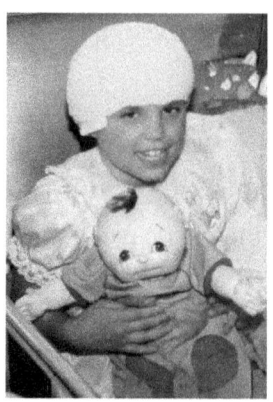

Helpful Resources

National Suicide Help Line
988 (call or text)

National Alliance on Mental Illness
741741 (text)

National Association of Anorexia Nervosa &
Associated Disorders
1-888-375-7767

National Alliance for Eating Disorders
1-866-662-1235

National Drug Helpline
1-844-289-0879

Relational Wisdom 360—
Going beyond emotional intelligence:
www.rw360.org

Table of Contents

Author's Notes iii
Helpful Resources v
Prologue 3
Chapter 1:
    Red Lights, Shattered Dreams & Reflections 9
Chapter 2:
    Kenny Rogers, Poker & Our Family Retreats 21
Chapter 3:
    Identifying Toxic Habits, Food
    & Relationships 29
Chapter 4:
    Bullies, Best Friends & Grief 43
Chapter 5:
    Space Camp, Hobbies & Meditation 53
Chapter 6:
    Fear, Detroit & Making Changes 61
Chapter 7:
    Alcohol, Addiction & Anguish 71
Chapter 8:
    Perseverance, Strength & Integrity 83
Chapter 9:
    Food, Grace & Neurotransmitters 91
Chapter 10:
    Pain, Fortitude & the Gospel 101

Chapter 11:
> Thoughts, Tightropes & Transformation 113

Chapter 12:
> The Phoenix Flies 123

Acknowledgements 135
About the Author 139
Other Books by the Author 140

*For if you remain silent at this time,
relief and deliverance for the Jews will arise from another
place, but you and your father's family will perish. And
who knows but that you have come to your royal position
for such a time as this?*
~ Esther 4:14 (NIV)

*Ask, and it will be given to you.
Seek, and you will find.
Knock, and the door will be opened to you.*
~ Matthew 7:7-8 (CSB)

Prologue

I almost died when I was five years old. I actually did, for a minute or two. Pieces of me never fit together the same way again. I had been a rambunctious, fearless kid. Glimpses of brief scenes from before the car accident sit at the edge of my memories. I remember jumping backwards off a picnic table, pulling my highchair down on myself, and climbing trees in the wooded area by my backyard. My days of gymnastics and carefree existence ceased to exist on Middlebelt Road in 1982. The lessons I have learned in the four plus decades since that day have often left more questions than answers. This is a journey to holistic healing. This is a story about me.

It is also a story about you. The confusion of chaos haunts us all through the events of life. This rollercoaster does not stop while we still have air in our lungs. Happy narratives, sad narratives, and frightening, shameful ones not yet ready to be shared. It is with profound respect for you that I write this book.

Carry each other's burdens, and in this way
you will fulfill the law of Christ.
~ Galatians 6:2 (NIV)

Live Life Courageously is not meant as a trauma dump yet there are difficult stories within these pages. Names have been changed to protect everyone involved. Locations remain true to the story for relevant context.

I grew up outside Detroit, Michigan in a community still affected by the riots of the 1960s. I vividly remember stories shared by the older generation.

My parents were quite young when they started a family. My grandparents were not intrinsically involved in our lives, as they were dealing with baggage of their own. Yet we were blessed with older neighbors and older church friends who guided my parents and offered them friendship and fellowship.

Mr. and Mrs. O'Hara were one neighborly couple that opened their home to us. Each time we went there, I was given explicit instructions. "Do not speak unless you are spoken to."

I remember listening to the adults as they played a game of marbles on the hand-carved board. I loved the smell and feel of the precious wood and the marbles that were in so many different colors I did not know even existed. I wanted one of those boards so badly, but Mr. O'Hara had made it by himself. There was no other.

The adults whispered with various intensity and when the pitch rose to a heightened level I strained to listen, desiring to know what they were talking about.

I was delighted when I heard my parents laugh, and surprised when new words were spoken. I came to realize that these new words were not kind ones for public use as Mrs. O'Hara chastised the offender, Mr. O'Hara, after their use. But the other adults at the table laughed in response, confusing my innocent mind. Eventually the shock and awe wore off, and I also giggled at Mrs. O'Hara's rebuke towards her husband.

Those early days, sitting in the neighbor's living room, fighting off boredom by playing with whatever toy I brought. My active imagination took over and suddenly I was not alone. Just alone with my thoughts.

This can be a place of peace or a place of torment. It all depends on the mindset I choose and to whom I am looking.

When I gaze upon the past with regret or defeat, I am not in a godly headspace. When I look towards the future with faith and hope, I am glorifying God with my mind and soul. Even if I still have questions.

May the God of hope fill you with all joy and peace as you trust in him, so that you may overflow with hope by the power of the Holy Spirit.
~ Romans 15:13 (NIV)

The explosion of life is evidenced by a multiplication of cells orchestrated by an invisible Hand of God and time marches on with exponential growth. The duplication is confounding. Cellular fabric is woven from threads of biological forces, circumstances beyond our control, and ideological constructs. From a baby's first cry to the final moments, the bookends of life stretch with millions of cells in between marching toward the same goal. Longevity.

The many systems of the human body generally work together to maintain function. Until there is a foreign invasion, abnormal growth, or an injury that cannot survive the insult. We make choices every day that result in an improvement or decline of our cellular matrix. Toxins in our environment, our food, our relationships and in our choice of relaxation build up over time. The tipping point is reality.

The purpose of life is more than a number on the scale, perfectionism, or adhering to religious rules. You love God, but you are tired. You have tried to be good, clean, holy, and all the things—and it is breaking you. Jesus' promise to carry our burdens can feel out of our reach during life's devastating trials. The journey to true healing is one that makes peace with the past, finds contentment in the present and faith in the future. We need to rediscover ourselves, ignite our true character, and allow space for redemption. We are not trapped in survival mode. We are survivors.

One look at a sunrise reminds me that God's mercies are new every morning (Lamentations 3:22-23). A glance at a smiling toddler reminds me of the miracle of life. Cuddling my 75-pound Weimaraner when I feel blue, seeing the look on her face that tells me she knows how I feel and is there for me reminds me of the purity that nature was intended to possess. Life's unpredictability cannot be explained yet I find my best resource when I approach God with open hands and bended knees.

The principles of excellence, wellness, and joy have guided my adult path. It is my prayer that we embrace them together as we strive to make positive imprints on our families, our communities, and our world. It only takes a spark to ignite change. We can be that spark toward transformation. This framework is reliable and encouraging but I cannot promise any results outside of the promises of God.

Kindling Courage

1. What event had the biggest impact on your life?
2. What values inspire you in your daily life?

3. How would life be different if you truly believed in the promise of Jesus from Matthew 11:28?

> "Come to me, all you who are weary and burdened, and I will give you rest. All of you, take up My yoke and learn from Me, because I am gentle and humble in heart, and you will find rest for yourselves."
> ~ Matthew 11:28-29 (CSB)

Chapter 1

Red Lights, Shattered Dreams & Reflections

I can still hear the impact. Metal-on-metal screech followed by a boom. These noises haunt me when I am not guarding my thoughts. Flashbacks pull me to that time threatening to paralyze future potential. And that is when I must remember that memories cannot hurt me. The tendrils of fear will not win.

> "Do not fear, for I am with you; do not be afraid for I am your God. I will strengthen you; I will help you; I will hold you with my righteous right hand."
> ~ Isaiah 41:10 (CSB)

The grace of God guides me through the challenges of life. No amount of religious discussion or regulations can ease the pain I feel in the darkness. Perhaps you have suffered empty platitudes during the struggle that have also depleted your spirit. Fear not dear one, there is comfort for your soul with the presence of the Holy Spirit. He is more powerful than any human construct.

As I sit down to share my story it almost feels like I am talking about someone else. In the four plus decades since that tragic day I have lived a dutiful life, accomplished much more than was thought possible by medical experts, taken chances, persevered, experienced setbacks, made mistakes, second guessed myself, and moved forward. To relive the past by sharing my story is difficult; emotions burst forth with painful flashbacks and memories. I spent a year and a half recalling these events, praying and crying while my fingers hit the keyboard, yet there is healing in stories and power in truth.

I am the girl who lived outside the Detroit city limits on September 20, 1982. Surviving a life-threatening event is a blessing that carries a double edge. This gift of life is splattered with a perplexity no one expects. When you are declared a "miracle," the implications of that statement are exponential. And yet survivor's guilt follows me like a shadow.

At five years old I experienced a traumatic brain injury (TBI) due to a horrific car accident. My babysitter, a grown woman from our church, and I were out garage sale (tag sale) shopping one day in her Escort GT (small car) just outside the Detroit city limits. She loved to spoil me with dollar knick-knacks and record albums.

I look at the traffic light as it changes from red to green ...

Crash.

Lights out.

I am standing in front of a line where people are standing in line to see me. I do not like the feeling it gives me. People are talking and I do not understand them. Someone is right beside me, but I do not know who.

"Jesus loves me, this I know.
For the Bible tells me so."

The physical impact of the motor vehicle fractured the right side of my skull, necessitating emergency brain surgery. The single neurosurgeon in the small hospital was moments from starting a critical operation from which he could not leave. The timing was perfect, a God-ordained distraction or a matter of chance coordinated events to save my life. I believe it was the former. To this day I have great respect for neurosurgeons. And not because of Dr. McDreamy, (with respect Shonda Rimes).

I open my eyes and see my mother waving at me as she came into a room with swinging doors. Men are kneeling just outside in a prayer position. I am confused.

I lay in a coma for 14 days after the surgery. Skull fragments were removed, leaving a baseball size hole in the right side of my head. My world sat on pause with my life quivering in balance. This pause created lifelong challenges and blessings.

While in a coma I was infected with a hospital acquired disease called pseudomonas meningitis. This aggressively dangerous disease affects the brain and is associated with a high fatality rate. The medical team advised my parents to keep their expectations low for my survival.

Hospital staff busied themselves with daily agendas attending to my bedside in order to check boxes. Regaining consciousness was a small part of the battle. The TBI, combined with the meningitis infection, attacked my nervous system with such force that I lost my ability to speak, walk, and care for my personal needs.

My mother stayed with me most days, leaving only for coffee or a quick lunch. Despite the hospital team's objections, my father stayed in my room at night, and they eventually provided him with a small bed.

Shortly after I regained speech my father advised my mother that he thought I was deaf in my right ear. She was visiting with me that day, having this conversation on the phone. I remember her handing me the phone in my right hand to speak with him.

Hello. Hello? Mom, he hung up. I handed the phone back to her.

Late one night, my father and I were awakened by a nurse who advised us that I needed to have another spinal tap. He stood by my side for this painful procedure, making up silly songs to sing and coaching me through it while holding my hand. After the procedure, he voiced his displeasure regarding the middle of the night waking to the entire unit sparing no words. I smile when I think of his temperament and protection. My sparkling disposition is no doubt inherited.

The year 1982 painted a collage of artistic expression. Madonna, Tootsie, Joan Jett, Christie Brinkley, MASH, and E.T. topped the charts in entertainment news. The movie Star Wars, featuring Darth Vader (introduced on the big screen in 1977), continued as a cultural icon. I thought Darth Vader was real. Real and terrifying.

Halloween was a celebrated event in the hospital. The first character to show up in my room that day after my mother left for her morning coffee break was none other than Mr. Vader. This frightening encounter had me scrambling to cover my head and hide. I pulled my intravenous (IV) line out in a state of fright. He then took his helmet off and I realized it was just a man dressed up.

A nurse came in soon after chastising me for making a mess.

Side Note:
The Hippocratic Oath should also advise against frightening small children recovering from brain injuries.

After a three-month stay, I was discharged from the hospital with physical, occupational, and speech therapy services. The next six months I worked hard learning to walk, talk, socialize, and regain bladder control. I loved my speech therapist because we played games. I argued a lot with my occupational therapist because she kept challenging my fine motor skills by having me string up small beads. My physical therapist always had a smile on her face and she created fun games. One day, my father came home with a book to learn sign language because he feared I would lose my hearing completely. This was my kindergarten playground.

Heightened vigilance marked the next three years of my life. I was petrified that I would hurt my head somehow and die. The adults around me constantly reminded me that I needed to be extremely careful with my head. Everywhere I traveled by car or bike an enormous ugly white helmet covered my head.

Fortunately, my physical therapy team recommended ballet lessons to help further my progression with walking, balance, and coordination.

Dancing gave me permission to be me. It was the one fun activity I participated in without the ugly helmet. The disabilities I faced became distant noises while I was on the dance floor. I welcomed the challenges of memorizing steps and balancing my body weight. Ballet pushed me out of my comfort zone into another zone of comfort where I was given permission to thrive.

Before the accident mother kept my hair short because I was a tomboy. After the first surgery I was allowed to grow my hair out. It grew back thick and was finally at a long length that made me happy.

I can still hear my braids being cut to prep for my second brain surgery at the age of eight. The scissors were my enemy that day. My long, beautiful braids were gone in minutes.

The purpose of the surgery was to replace the skull that was removed because of the initial injury; a procedure known as cranioplasty. Due to hospital team miscommunications, I was not given any sedation while still in my hospital room. They decided it would be best to take an anxious eight-year-old into the operating room by wheelchair. The operating room team was not prepared for the strong, fierce fight that I gave them. I refused to let go of my father. They had to gown him up around my hold and he had the unpleasant duty of carrying his daughter to the operating room suite. I kicked and screamed and clawed and hit as the team peeled me off him and held me down while the sedative was finally administered.

The highly anticipated repair was not without complications. The expected two-hour procedure turned into eight hours. An allergic reaction to a medication caused the operating room team to add resuscitation to the surgical procedure that day.

I woke up from anesthesia with the worst backache of all, the after effect of chest compressions. That evening a priest was sent for by the team. Through my blurry vision I watched him walk into my curtained area in the intensive care unit. He carried something in his hands. My head hurt and I was nauseous as I realized I was facing death. I knew enough about religious ceremonies to know the purpose of his visit. It was one of the scariest moments of my life.

> "It's not the size of the dog in the fight;
> it's the size of the fight in the dog."
> ~ Mark Twain

Over the next week the headaches became less intense, and my vision normalized. I was transferred from the intensive care unit (ICU) to a normal hospital room. My head was wrapped up in a multitude of white bandages, and I was anxious to see my head without them. When my mother finally agreed to let me see the bare skin on my head I remember laughing at the site of the operation because it looked like baseball stitching. My head had been transformed into a stitched baseball. Little did I know that children on the playground would have their own ideas of how I looked.

I could not always hear what they were saying but I learned to read lips and body language like a sixth sense. Hearing loss propelled my other senses into high gear. I became a quiet observer, learned to read lips, and developed a sense of discernment, for both environment and others. I discovered that my pulse could read the room quicker than I could verbalize it initiating me into a new skill set. I was exhausted by this amplified sense of awareness, and I found myself taking frequent hikes through the woods near my home to calm my soul.

The tension between a loving God and the tragic circumstance of life is not an easy dichotomy to understand. When we allow ourselves to see the good that can come from the ashes of tragedy, we open space for spiritual and physical healing. On the days when I focus on what I lost, I am stuck in a static state that will not change a thing. The cure is in acknowledging the blessings of God even when we are hurting.

Adapt, achieve, and overcome is the mantra my father preached with each struggle or setback during my recovery. I have translated this refrain into excellence, wellness, and joy. These principles are foundational pillars that foster success.

Excellence is a mindset choice. Adapting to our circumstances does not mean we have to accept them Rather, it is the opportunity to use our logic to outsmart them. Wellness is our ethical duty to care for our bodies. We achieve exercise goals, push our physical limits, and practice discipline. When we meet pain and failure in the gym, we know we accomplished something great! We found our starting point for the next day. Joy fuels our souls, allowing space for creativity, courage, and compassion.

Mind, body, and spirit are bound together like strands of a rope. Neglecting part of this human trinity depletes our ability to care for ourselves. The dance of life requires determination and tenacity to keep priorities straight. Sometimes it is a waltz, but often it is a tango. We adapt, we achieve, and we overcome.

> *Have mercy on me, Lord, for I am faint;*
> *heal me, Lord, for my bones are in agony.*
> ~ Psalm 6:2 (NIV)

Kindling Courage

1. What new or special skill set have you developed because of trauma or grief?
2. Share an example of how you have outsmarted your circumstances. Use #courageousthoughts #livelifecourageously #superpower if posting on social media.
3. What style of dance or music would you classify your life? Why?

Chapter 2

Kenny Rogers, Poker & Our Family Retreats

My love for the movie ***Six Pack*** (1982) first introduced me to Kenny Rogers. His character, Brewster Baker, intrigued me. He was tough, yet tender. Driven, yet not too arrogant to be humbled, eventually. During the car race scenes, I envisioned my father and me racing his 1968 Red Nova. I loved that car.

Mr. Roger's raspy deep voice filled me with peace in "Love Will Turn Your Around." Brewster Baker drew me in; he spoke to me in a fatherly way I could understand. And I wondered, how did he learn to drive racing cars? (This was before I knew about stunt doubles). Also, after the movie, did he live happily ever after?

Diane Lane's Character, Breezy, played the spunky soul I admired. She took care of her siblings like a mama hen. At that time, I also wanted a bunch of siblings. She was someone I wanted to emulate. Whatever happened to Breezy? I watched that movie until their faces and voices were imprinted in my mind.

The caution with which I was advised to live was my constant companion. The helmet I was forced to wear outside or while in a car for three years reminded me of the fragility of life. One hit to the head may kill me. I feared people, and life, in general after that fateful September day in 1982. Fantasizing about being a strong independent race car driver, dancer, actor, or fierce teenager eased my anxiety, but then left me feeling guilty for not being able to try.

One day while I was looking through my parent's collection of albums and eight-tracks, I noticed Kenny Rogers was on the cover of one, featuring his song, "The Gambler."

Music, like art, affects us individually. Different feelings and impressions are taken from each experience. We may look at Van Gough and feel nothing, or we may look at Monet and feel light, breezy, and calm as if we are walking by his pond.

When I found "The Gambler," the words struck me deep and hard even though I did not fully grasp them. With maturity, my understanding of the song and its implications for my life grew. Houston, we have contact!

Our family cabin retreat in the Upper Peninsula of Michigan was an important part of my growth and development. My parents purchased this tiny treasure after 1985. It became my new playground, and I was given permission to play outside like a 'normal kid.'

No more helmet, unless I was driving an ATV. No more disagreements about climbing trees or exploring abandoned buildings. Gone were the days of trying to hold back my thunder. Yet after three years of hypervigilance, the anxiety of another injury did not leave me.

I cautiously learned to raise a ruckus again. We rode hundreds of miles on our ATVs and even as my hand cramped with fatigue I pushed the throttle further. We raced over land and lakes on our snowmobiles and participated in friendly competitions against other riders. During one of our adventures, I flipped my ATV over and my father caught it just before it crashed on me. It startled me but once I learned I was not as fragile as Humpty Dumpty, a fresh wave of confidence washed over me. I learned to shoot a rifle, build a shed, and always look down at the inside of the outhouse toilet with a flashlight before sitting. You never know what creature may be lurking in there. I also watched with interest as the area hunters cleaned the animals they caught.

Steve and Jim were the sons of the older gentleman, Mr. Point, who lived in the trailer across from our retreat. They were a few years younger than my parents. My father listened carefully while either Steve, Jim, or Mr. Point instructed him on the preparation of meat and local hunting regulations. As I grew up, the sons also spoke of mischief and keeping out of trouble when Mr. Point was out of ear shot. We all shared many laughs with their stories and wild adventures.

Our pot belly stove kept the cabin warm but required a lot of wood. My father taught me about the different types of wood best for burning and even let me take a swing or two with the axe. In all honesty, this is a skill I still have not mastered.

There was no electricity or plumbing in the cabin. We drove to the neighboring town and filled our water jugs from the artesian well. This became a little more challenging in the winters when we had to park on the main road and walk two miles to the well. (Was it really two miles? I don't know. It felt like ten when we dragged the jugs back to the car).

At night our entertainment involved board games, books, and card games. Poker was my favorite. I felt like I was getting away with something while playing the game at the age of nine. My private school teachers would never approve. The cookie always tastes better when you are told you cannot have it. We initially played for matchsticks. Yes, you read that correctly. My parents refused to buy the plastic poker chips, stating they were not necessary for our games.

The rules of poker seemed straightforward to me, and

I quickly became confused as to why I could not beat my brother. Then I realized that he was lying about the cards he held in his hand. My belief about lying at that time was that it was a mortal sin. But the more I listened to the words of "The Gambler," the more I started to understand the game.

Towards the end of my high school years, this song conveyed wisdom beyond my years. We are each dealt a unique deck of cards in life. We also carry the responsibility of calling the play for each move we make or are handed. Like Daniel from the Bible, we need to be sober minded enough to read the writing on the wall. Do we take a stand, give up, walk away, or sound the alarm? Or do we let ourselves become distracted by all that is shiny and bright? If we are not thinking with intention, we are gambling with our minds every day.

The importance of a prudent analysis of each decision cannot be overstated. I cannot risk distraction by what is thought to be good. In our society we tend to mislabel things as being under our control. All ignorance is not bliss.

But seek first the kingdom of God and his righteousness, and all these things will be provided for you.
~ Matthew 6:33 (CSB)

Thoughts dance for attention, eyes look out in wonder, judgement or confusion, and muscles strain in soreness. Choices, opinions, options, decisions. Movement is either accelerated or hindered by how well we have cared for our bodies and minds. Are we sustaining life or destroying it?

Dr. Claire Lewicki, played by Nicole Kidman in ***Days of Thunder***, articulates it poignantly when she states, "Control is an illusion." In Dr. Lewicki's admonition to face reality with the character Cole (played by Tom Cruise) she effectively captivates the man whose pride led him to be reckless.

I have heard the warnings against having a prideful spirit preached from many church pulpits. It is one of the seven deadly sins according to Christian theology. I never thought I had an issue with pride. Yet lately I have reflected on my prayers and actions after experiencing loss, grief, or illness throughout my life and I realize just how much I have tried to manipulate God. I have looked like a good Christian but behind closed doors I have had some grueling arguments with God and have unapologetically told Him that He needed to do things the way I wanted them done. Pride touches every aspect of life.

When I approach situations with an open hand, I

surrender my will to God and this allows peace to flood my soul with wisdom. We are better equipped to choose faith over fear when we are being honest with ourselves and God. The gamble of self-sufficiency instead of relying on God's promises is a recipe for disaster. It can be hard to believe in God during struggles. But that does not mean He goes away or that He will not fulfill His end of the bargain.

> *Let us hold on to the confession of our hope without wavering, since he who promised is faithful.*
> ~ Hebrews 10:23 (CSB)

Kindling Courage

1. What one thing can you do to help guard your thoughts?
2. What have you mislabeled as being in your control? Can you give this to God in prayer?
3. How have you handled a situation in which you felt pride arise in your heart?

Chapter 3

Psychological Stress, Biology & Discipline

I attended a private Seventh-Day Adventist school until the middle of my 5th grade year. This afforded me the opportunity to make a whole new group of friends in a public school just months before starting Strong Middle School. What could possibly go wrong?

The new school was huge compared to my old one-room school. The children were loud, picked on each other like a swarm of wasps, and dressed differently than me. I was enrolled in classes that were foreign to me – formal physical education and art—and the school bell was so loud that it shocked what was left of my sensory system. I was placed in 4th grade basic reading and did not catch up with my peers until the 7th grade. When the other students found out about my limitations I became an easy target.

I remember the first time I was punched in the face by a female peer. It startled me more than anything else. She hit my left cheek, and I was just thankful she didn't hit the right side of my head. Teachers were notified and she was sent into the school for the rest of recess. The second time she punched me was a similar scenario. It was always out of the blue. I had no idea why this girl hated me. The third time she punched me she got me right in the nose. This one was spicy! And my nose bled. Our mothers were finally notified.

My mother was very upset. I did not like to see her upset and I was afraid that she was mad at me. She assured me she was not and told me not to worry my father over the incident. Before getting out of the car when we returned home, she gazed deeply into my eyes and said, "I don't want you to ever start a fight, but you better make sure you finish it."

It did not take long for me to act on this advice. My little cousin transferred to my school a month later from Detroit. I remembered the stories my aunt told me of her sheltering his small body as bullets rang through the streets of the big city. He was only in 2nd grade, and he was small. From the moment he started my school I made it my job to keep an eye on him.

At recess a few weeks later, I heard that another student was teasing him and trying to start a fight. That was not going to happen on my watch. I quickly made it my mission to discover the offending student. As I approached him and advised him that he would not be messing with my cousin that day or any day, he walked backward tripping on his own feet and fell on his bottom.

"I'm sorry," he said standing up. "I didn't know he

was your cousin."

"Now you know."

"I would never mess with the Jolly Green Giant's cousin."

"What?"

"You know you are the tallest person in our school, don't you?"

I looked around at the small crowd that had gathered. My cousin stood by my side beaming. I was still a little confused.

My cousin's apologetic would be offender smiled. "You know, like the Jolly Green Giant?"

We all laughed at that as I looked around. He was right. I was the tallest.

It was interesting to learn that although I was the target of my classmate's insults, other children were looking at me. The power of observation did not escape me at that moment. While the smaller students were looking to me like some kind of hero, the slurs of my peers became like background noise. I loved being the Jolly Green Giant.

I have rarely heard someone say that he or she liked the middle school experience. This is one of the most awkward phases of human development. Our bodies change in ways that are confusing and, at times, frightening. To all the girls whose mother did not have "the talk," I feel for you. I understand.

Admittedly I do not have any daughters of my own. Yet, as a member of the human female species, I can attest to what I wish "the talk" would have included. Biology, bullies, and bad boys. Age-appropriate tidbits each year starting at the age of five. Of course, that may have meant a less interesting read for you all now.

Carrie led the group of bullies that tainted my middle school years. Her gossip spread quicker than Entertainment Tonight. Each day was like an episode from the trendy TV shows of the era which portrayed a mean girl, only she never changed. Her vileness worsened with each passing year.

By the age of 13 I had made it five years without serious injury to my head. I did not have to end any fights because there were not any others to handle physically. With each passing year my interactions with my mother became less. I think the stress and trauma of my brushes with death caused her to bury her feelings. She threw her time and energy into business. She did what she had to do to survive mentally and emotionally; a fact I can understand.

Eating healthy was not a hot topic when I became a teenager. In an attempt to process my own psychological stress from the struggles with both disability and peers, I turned to food. It did not seem to matter how many prayers I prayed, how many Saturdays were spent at church, or my amount of youth group involvement. Dancing was not a consistent sport I could use to release my pent-up frustration; I tried track at school but after the humiliation from tripping over the hurdles I dropped out.

I drank a twelve-ounce Pepsi for breakfast, ate a serving of French fries for lunch, and then went home after school to eat snack food until dinner. Then I ate dinner. I consumed ice cream, cookies, and other snacks like it was my Olympic sport. I became an expert at hiding trash from snack wraps, burying them deep in the garbage so no one would be any the wiser.

I noticed my body changing and after watching a show on television, learned that if I made myself vomit the scale should roll back, which meant I could continue to eat with all the benefits of comfort. So, I did. I was surprised at how easy it was and with the determination of a teenager, I made myself believe that it was normal. The shame from overeating only lasted as long as it took to make myself throw up. This behavior stuck around for longer than I would like to admit. But it gave me a weird sense of control. Until I looked at the scale and noticed the pounds were not rolling off. My peers noticed my changing size and used it as a weapon against me. Little did I know, this was just the beginning.

As my middle school years came to a close, the physical education teacher challenged our class to run a mile. One whole mile. This was a humiliating experience to start as I was already known as the track drop out.

The boys in my middle school could be classified as either kind, or they ignored me. It was straight forward with them, unlike some of the girls who pretended to be my friend only to end up on team Carrie. But on this day, during the mile run, Patrick and his friends decided it would be funny to run next to me and mock me.

"Hey Jess," Patrick shouted as he caught up to me.
"What?"

"Why does everything jiggle?" He pointed toward my chest and then down to my thighs.

The boys burst out laughing and then ran ahead. This wave of teasing confused me. After three years were all the boys on team Carrie now? I immediately felt self-conscious and walked the rest of the mile, much to my teacher's dismay. She looked rather displeased as I crossed the finish line last. She called out the minute number in a disapproving voice. I did not care, I knew I could have done better.

I did do better. In my mind I beat Patrick. I did not cry. And now that I had seen his traitor's side, I would not forget.

The summer before I started high school my doctor checked my cholesterol level. He expressed concern to my mother, in my presence, about my size. She did not appear concerned. The results revealed a very high number and risk of a heart attack. Another failure in my mind.

I did not dare tell either of them that I had also been making myself throw up. The lab results and the number on the scale were signs to me that I could not even do that correctly. Much later in life I would learn that those affected by bulimia do not usually lose weight the way they expect.

"Discipline equals freedom."
~ Jocko Willink

Jocko Willink is an American author and retired Navy SEAL who has been awarded many medals for his service to our country. He is also the creator and host of The Jocko Podcast and has been featured in many media outlets. To list all his accomplishments here I would have to write another book. I stumbled on his podcast one day when I was researching leadership authorities. He values discipline, which I would expect from someone with his experience. His point of view regarding discipline is something I had never heard before.

Read his quote again. Let it settle into your mind and soul. In a pleasure seeking, pleasure priority society, how can this be? I mulled this over in my mind for days. If I say no to an extra candy bar, what am I free from? If I commit to exercising regularly how is that giving me freedom? If I pass on the last call at the bar, what does that have to do with freedom?

Saying no to the extra candy bar allows me the freedom from extra calories that will cause inflammation in my body and thwart my goals to be healthy. Exercising regularly gives me the freedom to march towards longevity with a stronger body and mind. When I say no to that last call, I am giving myself freedom to be more sober-minded and think clearly.

Choosing to drink water is one of the most beneficial things we can do. But I do not like to drink water. It is tasteless. It is boring. And it does not provide the immediate gratification of a cup of coffee, soda, or an alcoholic beverage. My body does not care how much I do not like it. My body still needs it. I know all the science behind the importance of hydration, yet I still must be purposeful in my decision to drink it. Water is the marathon beverage; its benefits are robust and sustaining but require replacement. We need self-discipline to grab a glass of water instead of a sweet drink.

Water is a macronutrient that provides energy, but not in the same way as caffeine. It improves metabolism, helps excrete and filter toxins, maintains skin hydration, decreases constipation, and improves exercise output. It also provides a better environment for electrolytes to do their electric magic. When the body does not have enough of this nutrient, dizziness, low blood pressure, fatigue, and a multitude of other complications may occur.

Our bodies are great at deciphering what we place in them. For by consuming, we are changed. The human body is a miraculous species that can process many foods, both nutritious and non-nutritious. There is a unique tipping point in all of us. We will malfunction after consuming too much of the wrong thing. Self-indulgence is selfish.

I always found it interesting that water makes up so much of the human body and that Jesus referred to Himself as being eternal water (John 4:14). We nurture our souls by trusting Jesus. There is a correlation between making choices based on instant gratification and making choices based on our goals. We choose freedom over instant gratification in order to live life with a strong mind, body, and soul.

Neglect of our bodily requirements clouds our spiritual clarity. The brain, the gut, and the skin arise from the same layer of fetal development which makes attending to each of these aspects with great care essential. They form an intricate trinity in that when one is malfunctioning the others will eventually follow suit. We honor God and our bodies by caring for each system with thoughtful actions.

> *But whoever drinks from the water that I will give him will never get thirsty again.*
> *In fact, the water I will give him will become a well of water springing up in him for eternal life.*
> ~ John 4:14 (CSB)

I often think more clearly when I write. There is power in the pen. Our healing requires recognition of the choices we make each day. Journaling is helpful in acknowledging challenges and brainstorming solutions. We make a commitment to ourselves when we commit to writing down our goals, the foods we consume, our prayer list, and our dreams for the future. It becomes an excellent visual for progress assessment and encouragement when we feel we are not moving towards our goals.

The saying "you are what you eat" is as true as "you are what you think." We need to nurture our mind, body, and soul to sustain health when challenges arise. Neglect of any part of this triad gives space to despair and destruction.

Living Water is the ultimate macronutrient for the mind and soul. Carry a water bottle and Bible every day to improve success. Reusable water bottles also make great gifts and stocking stuffers. Bible application downloads are free on your phone. These applications will even read aloud to you in different character voices!

Our health is multi-faceted, dependent on what we consume and what we think, how we talk to ourselves, how we feed our minds and how we feel physically and mentally. The secret to success with internal and external challenges is discipline. Yet society at large has made a spectacle of those who do not follow the breadcrumbs of self-indulgence. A pause before action, a thoughtful decision … these essential elements benefit humanity. A knee-jerk response to a trigger warning necessitates the reminder that triggers do not pull themselves.

When we care for our body, we are not selfish. We are glorifying God when we properly steward the life He has given us. Adequate sleep, participating in hobbies, exercise, and allowing yourself time alone are activities that nurture the mind. The busy body risks neglecting the mindbody connection. Thought patterns become cloudy and discouragement set in. This is when a season of spiritual dryness often appears.

Proper sleep is essential for proper thinking. When we are tired our minds are more susceptible to chaotic patterns and misunderstandings. This does not mean we are not "good Christians." It means we are neglecting our needs. The signals in our mental pathways become unable to respond to sensory stimulation and we either make rash, anxious, decisions or allow exhaustion to incapacitate. We become easily triggered or too exhausted to care about anything, even if our jobs require our attention.

Anxiety, fear, anger, sadness, flashbacks, or determination to solve a problem are a few of the internal issues that may also affect our sleep. Having honest conversations with God about these things may open the door to peaceful sleep. Honesty includes listening with an open heart and mind to any impression He may give. I learned a long time ago that He is the original night owl and likes to get my attention at 2 AM! Yet this is when the honest part becomes really good, if I am truly listening.

No one is perfect on this side of eternity; no man is an

island either. We need God and we need encouraging people in our lives. We choose our friends with wisdom, time is precious. Life is too short and valuable to waste energy trying to be someone I am not. The volume is turned down on the negative internal voices when we embrace the characteristics and abilities that God has given us. Like a ballroom dancer performing a solo turn, we keep our focus on where we want to go and find there is where our balance resides.

Finally, brothers and sisters, whatever is true, whatever is honorable, whatever is just, whatever is pure, whatever is lovely, whatever is commendable—if there is any moral excellence and if there is anything praiseworthy—dwell on these things.
~ Philippians 4:8 (CSB)

Kindling Courage

1. How has discipline given you freedom?
2. What is one self-care habit that you can incorporate into your week?
3. How can you change a negative thought into a life-sustaining thought?

Chapter 4

Bullies, Best Friends & Grief

With the start of high school, the talking points for the bullies at school went from "she has no brain" to "she is a slut" to "she is stupid" to "she is fat and ugly." I lost weight, but Carrie still called me fat. I wore very little make-up due to my father's strict rules, yet she still called me a whore. I am deaf in one ear, and she still called me dumb.

Our conflict peaked towards the end of the first semester of our freshman year. During a lunch recess Carrie lied to her friend, Ruby. Carrie told Ruby that I was still involved with her boyfriend. In reality, this boy had severed our relationship the prior month.

Ruby was furious. She confronted me in the local pizza parking lot with half the school as the audience. Carrie seized the opportunity to attack me for Ruby's honor. Fortunately for me, I was not alone in that fight. After Carrie's first swing at me, my best friend intervened, ending the fight that day.

The police and the court became involved in the aftermath of that incident. The amount of stress I experienced due to peer relationships, demands of school, all the opinions expressed by adults after the fight made me nauseous every day. I wanted to crawl under a rock and be by myself for the rest of my life. I was mentally and emotionally exhausted. I became moody and isolated myself from everyone. The hypervigilant state from prior years returned along with the belief that the world is not safe.

Due to this and other factors I did leave my hometown high school the following year to spend the remainder of my high school at a boarding school four hours away. I thought running away from my problems would solve everything. It did not. I returned home for my junior and senior years. Perhaps I can write further about that experience in the future.

The Lord is near the brokenhearted;
he saves those crushed in spirit.
~ Psalm 34:18 (CSB)

But then I noticed Eric. His smile made my heart flip, sending warmth through my body with a dizzying effect. He was standing next to Carrie but ignoring her and smiling at me. His white baseball hat tilted slightly to the side, a nod to the trend of the 90s. His eyes glimmered at me, avoiding Carrie's look of annoyance. In that moment, it was just us. Those eyes held my attention, sending warmth throughout my body, tempting me to get past my need for isolation.

Eric had transferred to our school a few months before, rumors were widespread about his mid-year transfer. Tongues spouted that he was the 'original bad boy,' or his parents were divorcing, and he had to move away from his terrible father, or he was an undercover for the police. The riskier the story, the more his popularity grew. I did not care about all the chatter.

He saw me.

Eric and I had a handful of exchanges during the time I knew him. Carrie made every effort to distract him. He would brush her off with a sigh and a shrug then walk toward me. Always a wink, then "hey." It was a level of attention that I was unaccustomed to. Lack of confidence, disbelief in myself and confusion left me almost speechless in our interactions. At least I remembered to smile.

We were in the school library the last time I saw Eric. He was without his usual entourage. My heart flipped when he approached. I couldn't move or speak but I smiled in return. He bent down, picked up a penny, and handed it to me.

"For your good luck," he said. His smile widened, he

tipped his head quickly, then turned toward the back of the library where his computer class assembled.

I stared in awe, unable to formulate a word. He acknowledged me. Not the deaf girl. Not the dumb girl. Not the slut. Not the fatty.

A few days after that interaction, on March 8, 1992, Eric was shot and killed. Carrie was furious with me when she saw me cry upon hearing the news. She yelled obscenities and threatened me before crumbling in the hallway. Her friends glanced back and forth as I fought to brave the walk away with my chin up, tears flowing down my face while my body trembled. I could not catch my breath.

My resources were limited. My best friend was in class. The school social worker was a moron at best. No one in his or her right mind spoke to the principle. I made it to the bathroom and lunged to the toilet as I lost my breakfast.

Grief is the elephant on the table. We see it yet do not want to talk about it. It provokes uncomfortable feelings – sadness, abdominal pain, nausea, insomnia, and hopelessness to name a few. The stress of grief can result in illness. Unsolicited platitudes do little to help. The soul is crushed with grief.

There is no shame in grief. Anyone that conveys otherwise is simply displaying a level of depravity that borders on evil. In response to the death of His friend, Lazarus, we find Jesus displaying grief. John 11:35 (NIV) is the shortest verse of the Bible and simply states, "Jesus wept." We see the humanity of Jesus displayed before the miracle. Jesus knew He could bring Lazarus back to life, but He still cried.

Our prayer life may check all the boxes. Our church attendance may be perfect. And we may have regular devotional time with God each morning. But the depth of confusion in grief can still hold us tightly. Mind, body, and spirit keep score. The mind and the soul jostle the matador's flag competing for attention. Our thought lives are at risk of spiraling in such times. And we must remember that we are never truly alone.

You will keep the mind that is dependent on you in perfect peace, for it is trusting in you.
~ Isaiah 26:3 (CSB)

The behavior of those around us affects us. Even more so with grief. It does not have to control us. It takes a unique set of skills to overcome the mess that life throws at us. Identifying lies and sharing struggles with a trusted friend is the beginning of healing. It can take hourly reminders to avoid internalizing the negativity.

The struggle against depression, anxiety, and addiction in response to events is real. Especially when you have held tight to strict religious standards and are taught that following God is all about what you can do for Him. Legalism does not help anyone, and it does not serve God. Our healing necessitates that we recognize and value the grace of God. He does not need you or I to do anything. He is God. He desires our love. He does not need it. I realize how uncomfortable this might make you feel. We will return to this idea later to dig further into the concept.

Our identity in Christ is a gift. We did not do anything to deserve it. When we focus on the Source of our identity, we are stronger. In the chaos that is anxiety, anger, depression, or grief, we can learn to control our thoughts and meditate on Him.

I have read the Bible more than once and know most of the stories well enough that I may be considered a "good Christian." This information does not take the pain, frustration, or sorrow out of my life. It does, however, infuse my soul with the knowledge that I am with Jesus; I am not alone. And this is all that matters. I cannot control the behavior of others or their reactions to mine. I can control my thoughts and my own reactions.

In ***The Obstacle is the Way***[1], Ryan Holiday highlights what is truly in our control: our emotions, our judgements, our creativity, our attitude, our perspective, our desires, our decisions, and our determination. Everything else is not under our control. Let this be the litmus test of your life. We control how we decide to react to situations, or we give that control to someone else.

And the peace of God, which transcends all understanding will guard your hearts and your minds.
~ Philippians 4:7 (NIV)

A peace and joy that is present even through struggles and pain is a salve to heartbreak and catastrophe. It is easy to turn to a bottle or other substance in response to such pain, such grief. Call it a normal reaction to an abnormal situation yet there is a better way. One in which we can be sober minded and maintain a steady trajectory of healing.

We can and must train our brains to recognize when they are not receiving proper signals or nourishment. The brain contains an innate mechanism that requires a little more attention in times of stress. When we lean into the

---

[1] Holiday, Ryan. 2014. *The Obstacle is The Way*. Portfolio/Penguin USA

Holy Spirit peace and clarity will follow. We always have access to the Spirit; cultivating a relationship with this Spiritual Being is essential.

We need to be on high alert and sensitive to any warnings that our conscious or gut perceives. We cannot afford to turn a deaf ear to these warning signals. We must think about what we are thinking about. A dose of caution in the things consumed by the eyes and mouth is prudent indeed.

We must pay attention to our stress levels and the reactions of our bodies to such times. Gut health is more than chemistry. It can be the mechanism that saves your life.

Mind, body, and soul. What affects one, affects them all. Daily affirmations can be a helpful way to "re-wire" your thoughts. The character Minnie Jackson (portrayed by Octavia Spencer) proudly showers her charge with daily affirmations in the movie "The Help." Her words provoke confidence and convey gentleness. "You is smart, you is kind, you is important." You are important. You are seen. You are heard.

"Repetition of affirmation of orders to your subconscious mind is the only known method of voluntary development of the emotion of faith."

~ Napolean Hill

Kindling Courage

1. The author states that "healing necessitates we recognize and value the grace of God." How do you think that this helps?
2. The biggest mental block holding me back from this chapter's advice is_____
   _____
   _____
   _____

3. Share your daily affirmations on social media #courageousthoughts #livelifecourageously #affirmations

Chapter 5

Space Camp, Hobbies & Meditation

The movie *Space Camp* arrived in movie theaters in 1986. A year after my second surgery. It was another movie that inspired me in childhood.

I lived on a dirt road in a rural area of Michigan allowing night sky to shine with the brilliance of stars with no light pollution to disturb the glow. My father bought me a telescope when I was twelve and I vividly remember the night we found Jupiter. Eureka! I wanted to "go up."

For years, I begged my parents to go to Space Camp. The final year that I would be able to go with my older brother, they finally let me go. He turned 18 years old while we were there, after that he would not be allowed in that student program. I was so excited when we got on the plane without our parents that I did not have room for any anxiety in my mind. Maybe our instructor would experience a malfunction like the one in the movie and we would actually go up!

The shuttle ride from the airport felt like an exasperating length of time. After we finally arrived, we were placed in our group. The seven other students were very friendly and told my brother and I about their hometowns of Texas, California, Ohio, and Costa Rica. I was initially suspicious of their kindness but as the days went on, I let my guard down a little.

The Texas brothers were very funny and boisterous, I do not remember what they said but they had us all laughing in stitches on multiple occasions. The girl from Costa Rica was very nonchalant as she told us about the snakes in her country that climbed trees only to fall on her or other villagers. The girls from California were kinder than my high school peers. And the guy from Ohio shocked us all with his savant like knowledge of aircraft. He planned to join the Navy.

The Multi-Axis Trainer (MAT) at Space Camp looked like an easy simulation as I stood in front of the Huntsville, Alabama facility. At that age of 15, I dreamed of being an astronaut or a fighter jet pilot along with being a professional dancer or soap opera actress. Movies like *Top Gun*, *Space Camp*, and *The Navigator* filled my mind with endless possibilities of flight. Little did I know that my disability would exclude me from flying jets for the military.

The Space Camp crew informed us that MAT was developed as a training simulation for astronauts. NASA developed it to teach crews how to handle the aircraft if it started to tumble in flight. Essentially management of pure chaos.

Our team of nine each took turns attempting to master the trainer. I watched each teammate before me, observing mistakes and conjuring up ideas of how I would master it my first time. After all, I was to be the first female fighter pilot. The confidence I held quickly faded after spending a minute strapped into the machine. It was difficult to bring MAT under my control, and I failed. Not only that, I was also left with a sense of embarrassment over my internal arrogance.

The tumbles we experience in life can leave us feeling much like we are in the MAT simulator. With our eyes open, our vision is blurred as life spins around us. Our hands are unable to control the trajectory. We do not always have enough strength or knowledge to still the trainer or calm the confusion in our minds or bodies.

The spectrum of struggles, chronic pain, disability, trauma, violence and grief opens old wounds yet provides space for deeper healing. It is discouraging when past hurts come to light again in our minds. And it is tempting to question our beliefs which can leave us feeling confused and guilty. Memories cannot hurt us but perseverating on the negative is destructive and impedes personal growth.

Struggle increases stress. Stress increases confusion

and fear. In this life, you will struggle, Jesus even warned us of this fact. And then He said "Be courageous! I have conquered the world." (John 16:33, CSB)

A balance of the mind, body, and soul better prepare us for the struggles of life. Our thoughts either sustain or destroy life. The importance of such cannot be overstated. Quiet time with the Almighty each morning is an excellent way to start the day. I cherish this time, but I know it does not guarantee a day without struggle. And I also know that it is not a requirement, it is something I can choose to do.

Even when I go through the darkest valley,
I fear no danger, for you are with me;
your rod and your staff—they comfort me.
~ Psalm 23:4 (CSB)

God created each of us with different desires and raw talents. Participating in hobbies is essential for holistic health. These activities decrease mental stress. They give our subconscious space and time to process while we experience enjoyment. We all need to have something that we do that brings us a healthy dose of pleasure and nourishment for our brains. This is essential for the spirit. Pursuit of an interest outside regular occupation for relaxation is linked to decreased rates of depression, increased overall life satisfaction, and increased problem-solving skills.

In my thirties I attempted to return to the dance studio, but I soon realized that the time commitment was too great when considering my career, demands of motherhood, and helping to grow my husband's business. I took this as an opportunity to participate in hobbies that could include my family or that I could do while my children and husband were involved in their extracurricular activities.

Our schedules become packed with job and family obligations causing the average woman to neglect this part of health. No one gets a trophy for becoming this kind of martyr. You are worth more. Take time for leisure even if it means waking up five minutes earlier.

Simple practices like journaling, spending time in nature, and listening to calm music can be considered hobbies and do not have to be time consuming. A good friend of mine takes ten minutes each morning for coffee and contemplation. Consistency will improve relaxation and give the mind time for thinking better.

Dr. Deepak Chopra may hold a different religious view than you or me, yet he shares wisdom about the importance of well-being, purpose, meaning, internal dialogue and physical health. I have read some of his books and articles, and I also attended one of his presentations. His thoughts on self-care are prudent advice for women and men.

In his book Quantum Healing[2], Dr. Chopra lists a few valuable Keys to Self-Care. He states that "through self-care a higher state of wellbeing is attainable." This refers to what I stated before about the subconscious having time and space to process events while our conscious is experiencing pleasure.

He encourages us to devote time and attention to personal growth. How we spend our precious free time matters. Daily routines need to include a "good diet and physical activity." Incorporate midday walks around the office or around your house. We need to allow our brains "to reset by introducing downtime several times a day." We step away from our chores, work, and the business of life to take a breath and re-group. Get to "know your inner world through meditations, contemplation, and self-reflection." It is my prayer that our thoughts move us toward sustaining forces, not destructive ones. "Gratitude and appreciation" are essential in our daily routines. And finally, we need to learn "how to love and be loved." The greatest gift is love.

---

[2] Chopra, D. (2015). Quantum Healing. Bantum Books. New York.

Dr. Chopra further states "mental choices originate the messages that change organs, tissues, and cells. If you want to see what your body will be like tomorrow, look at your thoughts and feelings today." If you have lost physical ability the hope for recovery may just reside in every cell of your body.

> *I will ponder all your work and*
> *meditate on your mighty deeds.*
> ~ Psalm 77:12 (ESV)

Meditation and yoga are helpful relaxation and exercise techniques. Speculation abounds in religious communities regarding these practices that we have learned from the Far East due to the relationship between them and the worship of false gods. Music, dancing, and other forms of art have also been utilized to worship false gods. The intention behind what we choose is really the heart of the matter.

Several Bible verses instruct us to meditate on God's word and His wonders. Using Scripture as a mantra as well as praising God, we meditate for His glory. The practice of yoga is a form of stretching and moving the body. When I attend yoga classes my practice involves prayer and meditating on God. Yoga participation improves mobility, relaxation, blood flow and relieves chronic pain. It also stimulates every branch of this major parasympathetic nerve that aids in our rest and digestion.

Rest in God alone, my soul, for my hope comes from Him.
He alone is my rock and my salvation, my stronghold;
I will not be shaken.
~ Psalm 62:5-6 (CSB)

Kindling Courage

1. What Bible verse do you have memorized that calms you during stress?
2. Do you currently participate in a hobby? If not, why? If it is because of time constraints, how can you carve out an extra five minutes of your day to participate in a hobby?
3. How do you think incorporating yoga or stretching in your daily routine would help you?

Chapter 6

Fear, Detroit & Making Changes

The bullying I experienced through middle school and high school left me feeling awkward in my ability to make friends. I did not actively seek out people. Sit-coms and movies of the day displayed teenagers having the best time of their lives in high school. I bought into the lie that I was missing out. This left me feeling anxious and rejected. The summer I turned sixteen I decided that I was going to be a little bolder and more courageous. I obtained a job at an A & W carhop close to the Detroit city limits.

I do not remember their names, but I do remember their kindness. Two teenage boys, a couple years older than me, came to A&W one day for lunch. They had nice smiles, were very respectful while placing their order, gave me a great tip, and kept their area clean. They returned the next week and invited me to a party in Detroit.

"You gotta come with us and hear this guy. His rapping is so good. He's gonna make it big."

"I don't usually listen to rap music," I said with a smile. "But if you say he's good …" I raised my left eyebrow.

"He's great. They say his name is um," the passenger inhaled his cigarette, "I can't remember. It doesn't matter. They say he's gonna be big!"

Arrangements were made and they picked me up at my house then drove into the city. Detroit was no stranger to me. I volunteered there in a soup kitchen with my church, saw *Brigadoon* and *Cats* at the Fox Theater, attended multiple Red Wings games, drove around the city with my driver's training instructor, and had a few lunches at the Renaissance Center.

The neighborhood we drove into was well kept. Cookie-cutter raised ranches and colonials lined the road. Our destination proved to be crowded with cars in the driveway and lined down the road to the entrance of a park. It was not a proper park entrance, but the large open space of green grass was well lit with a baseball field at the other end.

We entered the house to find small groups of people crowded in the living room on couches, windowsills, and the floor, sitting on the nearby staircase and in the doorways. The house smelled like a mixture of skunks and mold. A young man with dirty blonde hair caught my eye. He had an intense look as he walked around talking to some, ignoring others. As he approached, butterflies filled my stomach.

"Hi," he said.

I was speechless and looked at the guys who brought me to the house. My eyes pleading for them to say something.

"She's kind of shy," the one interjected.

I took a deep breath only to have my lungs assaulted by the smell of smoke and marijuana. I coughed.

The stranger nodded, his gaze unrelenting. "Well, I'm gonna go do my thing."

I nodded as if I knew what he was talking about.

He walked to the middle of the room and started rapping. People quickly noticed and quieted. He dropped a beat new to my ears, the rhythm pulsing through the room, and his words crisp and catchy. I was surprised to hear music like that. It was not the rap I knew.

The music carried me away and I was distracted, unaware of my surroundings. Until someone handed me a bong. (This was decades before marijuana legalization, and I was not one to break the rules.) Fire bells and whistles went off in my head as I passed it quickly to the next person. My heart pounded and I was nervous. I looked around and couldn't find the guys that brought me to the party.

Part of my brain beckoned me to partake, escape my fear, settle in, and listen. Maybe it would be fun? I might just have a great story to tell someday. The logical part of my brain disagreed, and fear filled my mind. What if the cops came? My parents would be furious with me if I got in trouble and I did not want to be sent back to boarding school.

My feet took over, and I found myself outside the house. I looked around and still couldn't see anyone I recognized. Through the front window I could see the rapper continue his song. Feeling awkward just standing on the porch and not wanting to go back inside the house, I started walking. The well-lit park was welcoming with its manicured lawn and wide-open space.

I made it to the other side of the park by the time my absence was noticed. One of the guys came running toward me, a worried look on his face.

"What are you doing, hon?"

"Walking." I smiled and looked at him.

"I see that. But this is Detroit." He stepped in place with me.

"Yes, and this is a beautiful park."

"Why'd ya leave the house? Don't you like his music? I was worried when I couldn't find you."

"He's got a different beat. I like it. But I didn't know there was going to be drugs there. I just don't like that stuff."

"Oh. I'm sorry."

"No, I'm sorry. You can go back in and listen. I'll be fine walking."

"But it's Detroit."

"I've heard about this city," I giggled.

"No. We'll take you home."

We walked back to the house, found his friend, then they drove me to my home. They were both gentlemen about the whole evening. We joked and laughed on the way back to my house. They kept commenting on the crazy white girl who went walking in a park in Detroit by herself at night. Those two boys probably saved my life that night. I wish I remembered their names. If either of you are reading this, thank you.

The night could have ended tragically. As I reflect on my teenager fear of missing out (FOMO) I realize that it was a dangerous decision. I am also aware that FOMO is an adult issue I juggle as well. When I attend an event that will go late into the night, and I know the next morning I have important responsibilities, is the FOMO worth it? We must analyze our choices in relation to the life we desire to make the best decisions. Life is not something to gamble.

Fear of missing out can take on many forms, like tasting a new food or beverage, a promised fun night, a bit of gossip, or a new form of entertainment. FOMO has a wide variety of implications physically, mentally, and financially. It can also have disastrous consequences. When we are alone with our thoughts are we moving towards sustaining or destructive forces? FOMO is not a reason to do something. Wisdom prevails when our thought lives are disciplined. And remember, discipline is not depriving ourselves of something, it is taking control of our life so that other things cannot control us.

Discipline is also closely related to healthy boundaries. Holistic healthy boundaries involve the mind, body, and soul. We need to consider carefully the sensory stimulation from television to social media that we allow our brains to witness. When we set personal guidelines for ourselves and how we expect to be treated we are better able to care for our needs and the needs of those we desire to be a part of our lives.

Fear breeds fear, anger breeds anger, hurt people will hurt people.

I sat on the floor of my living room, playing a game with my 10-month-old son on the morning of September 11, 2001. My mother called and told me to turn on the television. The unspeakable tragedy played out before me. Tears ran down my face as a wave of nausea passed through my body. My uncle was in New York City.

Days passed. We received news that my uncle was safe, but I kept watching the television, and I kept worrying. The tag lines and suspense kept me on high alert, believing that any second an event would again change the landscape of our nation.

My thoughts flashed back to witnessing the first Gulf War from my grandmother's trailer park in Florida. I watched as missiles were deployed throughout the night in a foreign country. Was that going to happen here?

Media has a strange influence on the mind. With one short news story I felt hopeless and then anger provoked me to do something, like I could change the world, and everything in between. My mind was distracted during the day with the letters I should write, the number of supplies I should stockpile, and how if I just spoke to the right person maybe things would go back to normal. In my fear, I went to the ultimate fix-it mode.

In his book ***Meditations***, Marcus Aurelius rightly points out, "It's time you realized that you have something in you more powerful and miraculous than the things that affect you and make you dance like a puppet."

In a spiral, my fear sparked another fear that made me believe I could and needed to control everything. I found myself preoccupied with anger and grief while trying to navigate the role of a young mother and wife. One day, exhausted from the emotional roller coaster and the negative energy fed by continued screen time, I decided to turn the news off and return my attention to God instead of the media. I cannot take credit for this decision alone. My father called and told me to turn off the news.

Mind boundaries (emotional and mental boundaries) are essential. I think I now know the limits I need to set for myself to thrive. These limits are not necessarily your limits. Distinguishing good from harmful is wise (and highly recommended) when it comes to your mind. This is a skill that requires a fully functional frontal lobe in our brain (this occurs around the age of 25) and practice. I would argue that people under this age need more loving guidance than is common in our current time. And, as a society, we need to be less enamored with the decisions of the youth. If you have not yet read *1984* by Orson Wells, now is your time.

> *A fool does not delight in understanding*
> *but only wants to show off his opinions.*
> ~ Proverbs 18:2 (CSB)

When friends and family do not understand your desire to change a habit, hold true to your goals. They may try to talk us out of it, they may be afraid we will try and fail, or they may not like the tension it causes for them to change. The intention behind their feelings is irrelevant. It is an unnecessary distraction. Friends may leave you; family may argue with you; these are never comfortable situations. You are not alone. I am cheering you on from the pages of this book!

To start the process of change before telling others is often wise. Imagine if you quit drinking alcohol a month before anyone knew? Or imagine if you ran a 9-minute mile before anyone knew you were training? You are already developed in your goal far enough to avoid the pitfalls of peer pressure.

Life has been likened to a highway, a journey, a roller coaster, and a path. In my opinion it is best thought of as a game. How well we play this game determines our success. An excellent mindset will outsmart the circumstances that tell us there is no time to exercise. A wellness mindset outwits the thoughts that lead to unhealthy choices. A joyful mindset embraces our soul with peace and perseverance.

Games should be fun, and so can our commitment to health. It does not mean that it is not hard work; in the end the fun comes from using creativity in obtaining goals and allowing yourself to enjoy God's blessings through it all. A healthier version of us provides our families with the opportunity of dealing with our sparkling personalities longer! Yes, you have one too!!

Set your minds on things above, not on earthly things.
~ Colossians 3:2 (CSB)

Kindling Courage

1. Fear of missing out can take many forms. What does it look like in your life?
2. How has the media affected you negatively? How has it affected you positively?
3. Would you ever be willing to take a day off of using social media? A week? A month? Why or why not?

Chapter 7

Alcohol, Addiction & Anguish

He may have been attractive had there not been blood dripping down his chin and onto the floor of the bathroom when I met him. The 49-year-old man admitted to the hospital for alcohol detoxification looked at me with confusion and pain in his eyes. My 18-year-old mind jumped into high gear forcing my fear aside as I pushed myself forward. I was the only nurse's aide available to help him. This was my initiation, as the old saying goes, a 'baptism by fire.'

I will never forget the look on his face, pleading for help as I wiped the blood from his chin and neck. With his roommate's assistance I led the man back to his bed, turned him onto his side then raised the bed rail. He mumbled softly as I left his room to alert the charge nurse and change my scrubs. He was transferred to the intensive care unit (ICU) and did not survive the night.

Alcohol intake affects every cell in our bodies. Excellence cells, wellness cells, and joyful cells. These tempting beverages can literally change our lives! The "power" packed empty calories, sugar and fat content, and other foreign chemicals result in anything from blissful ignorance to raging madness, with a form of dementia in between. It also impedes our weight loss goals as the calories and subsequent inflammatory response builds up in our bodies.

A "guilty pleasure" can quickly (and easily) lead to a daily habit which then welcomes addiction. It takes strength of mind and a strong support system to avoid the consequences of frequent alcohol use. Alcoholic encephalitis is terrifying from the bedside; I cannot imagine that it is any less scary for the one who endures it.

High carbohydrate intake will increase our body's serotonin levels but sometimes this is not enough. When an escape is needed from the whirlwind of emotions, crazy scheduling, and the tragedies of life, a handful of potato chips may not suffice. In those times I am tempted to isolate myself again and seek immediate, yet short-life, gratification.

I have learned to surround myself with people I know who share my values that I can call on at any time. I do not avoid spending time with people who do not share my values, life is sacred, and I respect different opinions. Yet I know the few that I can count on to walk with me through chaos and call me out on my own issues when needed. This is a healthy balance. A friend that always agrees with me may not be paying attention.

God grant me the serenity to accept what I cannot change, the courage to change what I cannot accept, and the wisdom to know the difference.

~ Reinhold Niebuhr

"Whatever you do tonight, don't start drinking." The Chief of Police said to me.

I looked at the officer as my vision blurred with tears. The sound of my neighbor shouting for someone to call 911 echoed in my mind like a thunderclap. I had jumped into action, my training and experience as a nurse took over as my attention went to the small lifeless body on the pool deck. I frantically looked around for my children as I started performing cardiopulmonary resuscitation on the two-year-old. I quickly made eye contact with them before another neighbor whisked them away. My young sons, ages 3 ½ and 6 ½ had a front row seat to the tragedy. I can still feel my neighbor's hand on my back as he led a small group of others in prayer while I counted each chest compression, the rhythm steady under my hand.

I sat with the Chief inside his car, having just given my statement, as the tears rolled down my cheeks. "I'm serious, Mrs. Fett. Do not drink. It will not help you."

I took a deep breath and nodded, turning my head toward him. His face was kind and full of compassion, but firm. He spoke with wisdom and experience beyond my years. And he meant it. His eyes pleaded with me to trust him with this instruction.

"Do you have anyone who can stay with you tonight?"

"My husband is out of town for business." I stared at the used Kleenex in my hand. "But my mother is here. I'll be fine. Thank you. I have to go check on my kids." I glanced at the officer one more time and gave a weak smile before shutting the door.

It has been almost twenty years since that day and I still reflect on his advice, especially during difficult times. That day I followed his instructions. And sadly, there have been other occasions that I have not. I have let pride infuse my mind into thinking that a few of this or that will make everything better. The porcelain throne and I have become well acquainted through the years. Yet, I continue to learn, to pray, and to trust in God, even through hardships and my mistakes.

Turning toward alcohol or any substance in times of strife or tragedy makes it even more challenging for the mind to process events and turn toward helpful resources. Substances inhibit our ability to process events and verbalize our needs. They also interfere with our ability to take any advice. Alcohol is a natural depressant thus turning towards it in a time of sadness will only increase our anguish. And this is when things can get very, very dangerous.

Addictions come in a variety of forms, but they all serve the same purposes. Escape and reward. We seek escape from grief, anger, and anxiety. We think we need to remove ourselves somehow from life and that the reward will be an anticipated pleasure. The addiction attempts to compensate for fear then tricks the mind with false hopes of obtaining the ultimate prize.

The reality is that the stakes eventually need to be raised to achieve the rush. Instead of feeling good gossiping about one friend, pride eventually takes over until we are gossiping about everyone. Word gets around and our reputations are destroyed. After weeks of consuming two drinks of alcohol, our systems are dulled to the initial effect, and it becomes a daily habit. Precious time is lost to an ingested chemical; time that cannot be retrieved. Fear of being unloved leads many to sexual experiences that necessitate more partners, real or virtual, to calm the inner distress.

The insecure (fearful), angry, and sad voices in our minds are all too ready to hold us back. The struggle to not internalize the lies spewed by this negativity is overwhelming. This is a major cause of the mental health and chronic illness crisis in our society. The National Alliance on Mental Health (2021) reports that 22.8% of adults experienced mental illness (that is 1 in 5 adults), 5.5% of these cases were considered 'serious,' and 7.6% of have also experienced a substance use disorder.[3] We have allowed negative thoughts to captain our personal ships. And the children around us keenly watch.

Anger is an umbrella term for many negative emotions, yet it can also be a positive reaction in the face of injustice or harm. How we react when we are angry matters. When left unchecked, anger overtakes the soul. Buddhism notes that anger is one of the 3 poisons of the mind along with fear and foolishness.[4] The writer of Proverbs takes this further, lending some helpful advice, "He who is slow to anger is better than a warrior, and he who controls his temper is greater than one who captures a city" (16:32).

We are angry because we are hurt. We see injustice, feel it personally, and our inner selves roar with rage. We are angry because we cannot control everything. Failing at a task, we turn anger on the self. Depression, anxiety, and chronic illness are siblings to anger, not distant cousins.

---

[3] National Alliance on Mental Illness (NAMI), www.nami.org
[4] National Institute of Health Journal of Medicine and Life 2010 Nov 15; 3(4): 372-275 "Anger and Health Risk Behaviors" Staichu, M.L. and Cutov, M.

Anyone of these can initiate the cascade. My reaction to these emotions requires contemplative preparation.

Am I to use my emotions to start a riot in the streets or to become more knowledgeable about issues, educate others, and organize peaceful grassroots movements that spark change without hurting others? Educating ourselves in lieu of jumping to one sideline is a discipline not often chosen.

Do we use our anger to have an adult temper tantrum that results in property damage or to use the power of the pen to effect change? Is anger our excuse to turn to substances, or take a stand for our health and commit to utilizing exercise to blow off steam?

Our emotions pull us into a state of exhaustion that leaves us incapacitated. Anger increases our stress hormones[2] which lead to a constant state of 'fight or flight' draining our already limited resources. Our minds spin like the turning of a hamster wheel and we suffer from brain fatigue.

Think of the rust that builds up on an old car after driving on wintry roads full of salt for a decade. That rust is just like what can build up in our bodies when we are neglecting them. Chronic illness is the rust in this analogy. Increased rates of heart disease, gastrointestinal issues, insomnia, stroke, and headache plague those who struggle with untreated anger [5]

The next time we are angry, we need to search for the root of the cause. Epictetus said, "What is mine is mine, and what is not, is not." He believed that these were the only thoughts required. From a Stoic perspective, anger has no place in the thoughtful mind. Why be angry if something is not in your control? It is not a reflection of your character … it reflects whatever is controlling it. To ease the uneasiness and feeling of lack of control with anger, many have turned to alcohol, another substance, or violence. A combination of all of these is a deadly storm indeed.

In my research on the topic, I found that Harvard Health recommends five key strategies to overcome addictions. These require a commitment to self and desire to prioritize our health above all our feelings. Journals can also be helpful during these times to document and process struggles, milestones, and setbacks. Behavior patterns provide revelations.

Set a date and stick to it. Circle it on your calendar, tell a supportive friend and add it to your daily mantra. "On [date] I will no longer [add in specific addiction]. I will be healthier; I will be happier; I refuse to be afraid." We add our individual needs and desires into our mantras

---

[5] Better Health Channel (www.betterhealth.vic.gov.au)

to validate them.

We change our environment to remove any offensive substances, people, meetings, or agendas. We outsmart our circumstances when we can decrease access to temptations. If I am trying to quit smoking, I do not carry a pack of cigarettes in my purse. Small changes in our environments pave the way to our success.

Distractions are necessary to help fill the perceived void left behind. Many of my clients chew gum regularly, participate in a creative hobby, or immerse themselves in a new skill. The power of faith in God to help overcome addictions cannot be overstated. I have heard some preachers simplify the complex problem of addiction to the detriment of congregation members. Side note: I believe this is with good intentions and a naïve sense of the issues.

We need God AND we need supportive people to surround us with love and resources. It is not a "one or the other" option. In God alone is our salvation. I am not advocating for a salvation gospel that preaches we need God plus something else. Yet when we see our friends or family struggle it is our God ordained responsibility to support with love and whatever resources we have at hand. A support network of like-minded individuals that care for us is essential. We have every right to weed out the people

in our lives who are hindering our goals if they continue to place barriers to
change in our path. This is not selfish; it is life sustaining.

Journaling through the process to reflect on success is a great motivator. No attempt to quit is made in vain yet reality must be kept in sight. Perseverance is splattered with failures and new beginnings. Each time we fail, it is one less time we need to fail again due to the lessons we can learn from experience.

Relationships are sacred privileges. The relationship we have with ourselves is no different. The golden rule of treating others as you want to be treated stands the test of time. We need to also remember to treat ourselves that way we want to be treated. The ability to learn to quiet the inner negative voice, calm the surrounding chaos, patience, and a fully functioning brain. (See previous chapter regarding frontal lobe development).

There is a balance to sharing our time with others and with ourselves. Extroverts and introverts benefit from honest reflection on commitments to better discern when to say "no" to an invitation. We do not need to participate in every activity that we are invited to attend. Consider if the event is one that will increase stress to a point that is not helpful. When it is unhelpful or toxic, we owe it to ourselves to bow out with grace.

Family commitments may be looked at under the same lens. The line between appearing selfish and setting healthy boundaries with our family can be blurred. At the end of the day, we do not deserve to be the target of emotional toxicity by others because they are related to us. It is not wise to continue to expose yourself to toxic relationships and think that you can remain unscathed. Sometimes turning the other cheek is 'live and let live' from a distance.

Time is precious. Boundaries are healthy. Walls have been given a bad reputation in the context of building a wall around our hearts to not let others in our lives. Yet healthy boundaries are good walls that we set up so that we are not harmed in our mind, body, or soul. They are like shields of armor that thwart the arrows of toxicity.

Therefore, submit to God.
Resist the devil, and he will flee from you.
~ James 4:7 (CSB)

Kindling Courage

1. Based on the advice in this chapter, what is one thing you can do to help you move closer to holistic healing today?

2. Are you struggling with an unhealthy habit? Alcohol/Food/Smoking/Laziness/Swearing/Reckless Behavior/Other?
3. What is one boundary you can set up to help change this habit?

Chapter 8

Perseverance, Strength & Integrity

In his book ***Discipline is Destiny,*** Ryan Holiday advises "work hard, say no, practice good habits and set boundaries, train and prepare, ignore temptations and provocations, keep emotions in check, endure painful disabilities."[6] We are all responsible for our bodies, and some have bigger challenges to overcome than others. It is not fair. I can choose to push forward or give up. It is my choice if I am sidelined.

Life is messy, complicated, and not fair. Circumstances do not care about our individual situation. There are no special trophies or entitlements for the hand we are dealt. We thrive when we keep doing the next thing. Perseverance pays off.

"Once you're done praying get off your knees and start doing." ~ Grandpa George

The traumatic brain injury left me with weakness and muscle atrophy in my left leg. Sometimes I don't even

---

[6] Ryan Holiday, Discipline Is Destiny: The Power of Self-Control (New York: Portfolio/Penguin, 2022).

know where my left foot is positioned. I would like to believe that this has given me more opportunities to trip with grace, but who am I kidding? It is still a clumsy event. Yet I have learned to get up quickly in hopes that no one witnesses the catastrophe, as I limp away swallowing my shallow pride.

From Cross Fit training to Pilates or running and cycling to dancing, this weaker leg is a constant. Persistence is the only thing that allows for change. A little bit stronger, a little more balanced, a little at a time. Consistency is the champion of goals.

My first day of graduate school at Duke University included a lecture from the Dean of Nursing. She was witty and did not hold back when speaking of how our lives would change in the next few years. The proverbial rubber meets the road speech. Long study hours, sacrificing family time and sleep would be our new normal.

"You've spoken to your families about continuing your education and they may have given you glorious affirmations that made you feel good. That is over now. It is time to work."

Talking about how we want to change our thoughts and bodies to be healthier is more fun than putting in the effort. I can talk about plans all day long, sharing details with anyone who will listen. I exercise the strongest muscle in my body with talk, but it requires action to be powerful. Words float in the wind, actions change.

There are days when I do not want to exercise, eat properly, or even spend quiet time in devotion. These are the days when the line between commitment and giving up is very thin. We must take heart and reach into the Spirit Who lives inside us for vitality to thrive and endure.

Repeat your affirmations or mantras: discipline requires self-talk, self-motivation, and goals. Rise up.

"No man is free who is not master of himself."
~ Epictetus

"I do believe; help my unbelief!"
~ Mark 9:24 (CSB)

Prochaska and DiClemente[7] (P&D) developed a model that reflects the stages of change. The academic name of this model is The Transtheoretical Model. I first learned about this in undergraduate school. At the age of 19, I did not understand how hard it is to change behavior, and I did not appreciate having to learn something that I

---

[7] LaMorte, Wayne W. 2022. The Transtheoretical Model (Stages of Change). Boston University School of Public Health. Behavioral Change Models. www.sphweb.bumc.bu.edu accessed on Nov 22 2024.

did not think was applicable. Of course, people would want to change, I thought. I could not fathom why someone would not change for the better. Now that I am closer to my fiftieth birthday, I can appreciate the resistance to change a little more.

Stubborn lies about health paralyzes the ability to change. The drink is not good for the alcoholic, but he says, "just one more." The excess calories are not good for the diabetic, but she says, "I just can't stop eating brownies." Promiscuous relationships are not good for the lonely teenager, but she says, "I just want someone to love me." Salty snacks are not good for the one struggling with hypertension, but he says, "It's just a little snack." Our thoughts control our behaviors, and we will never find the courage to change when we allow lies to sabotage our goals.

I love the movie ***G.I. Jane***! Lieutenant Jordan O'Neil, portrayed by Demi Moore, epitomizes someone who spoke about her desire and took action. She pushed herself to the limit, striving for excellence and wellness to achieve her goal. Warnings and hard work did not scare her. Her mindset did not waver. Despite being deceived, alienated, and assaulted, her integrity and persistence did not waiver. In the end, her joy was in victory over the odds that were stacked against her. Joy is not guaranteed instant gratification of our pursuits, but it is the prize in the marathon of wins.

Carpe diem. Take your unique God-given strength inside of you, put it into action, adapt, achieve, and overcome. You can be the spark that ignites the next positive change for yourself and for others.

God gifts us with different characteristics, desires, and talents. When I try to fit into the mold of someone else, I am being prideful thinking that God did not make me the right way. We all possess a superpower of sorts. It is worth the time to reflect and train until we ignite transformation.

In his book, **Think and Grow Rich**, Napolean Hill pens an astute philosophy on desire. Almost a hundred years ago, the United States rose from the despair of a world war followed by a great financial depression. Desire was a luxury many could not fathom in the daily feat for survival. Mr. Hill recognized that desire creates space for imagination and hard work. Increase the desire for change and it will surely happen. Not because people like you or because you are pretty. But because desire fuels your body for action.

I recently watched a news piece about a town that was devastated by a tornado. The high school football coach was a man of faith, honor, and integrity. He valued community first and lived by example. After the storm, he gathered his team together and arranged for the cleaning and repair of the field and school. Knowing that football was a major community event and that restoring the space in time for the first game of the year would inspire and encourage the town folk, he charged the young men with the task of rebuilding.

This coach knew that he could not do it all by himself, but he knew it needed to be done. It was not his job, and it was not the job of the high schoolers. The coach knew the town, and he knew football. So, he kept doing the next thing until he could get back on the field and do his job. His example improved the lives of those in his community and will have a lasting impact as the students share his story with the next generation.

The value of dedication to a life of perseverance benefits us individually, our families, and our communities. People are most often remembered because of their actions, not their words. Unless they are famous writers. (Will you remember me?)

It is not about straightening your crown. It is not even about making your crown. It is all about participating in a meaningful relationship with the One who gave you the crown. He is not a set of rules, he does not require perfection. When we believe in the sacrifice of His Son as our Savior, we are made perfect. Jesus' sacrifice on the cross for us does not make sense from a human perspective, either. Yet it highlights His desire, not need, for our love. How many people do you know would die for millions of people that are not even born yet? Faith in God is trusting in Him and His plan through good times and bad. It is not always easy. It is a soul exercise in perseverance.

> *Do not conform to the pattern of this world but be transformed by the renewing of your mind.*
> ~ Romans 12:2 (NIV)

Kindling Courage

1. Do you feel paralyzed by circumstances of life, or do you keep doing the next thing to achieve your goal?
2. If you feel paralyzed, are you able to identify what is holding you back and place boundaries to get unstuck? Stubborn lies/fear/lack of desire?
3. Share your why for "doing the next thing" on social media. #livelifecourageously #DTNT #couragetochange

Chapter 9

Food, Grace & Neurotransmitters

Through my years of working with clients in private practice and community centers as a Family Nurse Practitioner (FNP), I have had the opportunity to get acquainted with individuals from every walk of life. My experience has been multi-cultural and multi-disease focused. I have experience with each medical specialty in some regards.

Giving someone a label, telling an individual she has a disease is no easy task. This requires a skill set that I wish I did not possess. Because in a perfect world, I would never have to learn how to tell someone they have cancer or the human immunodeficiency virus (HIV). There is a kind, compassionate way to relay this information that not all medical providers possess. It was not something that I was taught in school. It was something that I had to learn. And the first time I did it, I messed up big time. You always remember the first time.

The following story contains some pearls from the field. Missy is a patient who stands out in my mind. She was a hard worker, had a sparkle in her eyes, and a single mom. I think about her often as I learned from her as well.

Missy sat and stared at me, silent tears betraying her mood in response to the laboratory tests we just reviewed. A single mom with two toddlers, she was overworked, overstressed, and not sleeping well. Half of her paycheck went to pay for childcare. She had not been to the doctor since the birth of her youngest.

I waited patiently, not sure if I should pat her shoulder or cry with her. It was a busy day in the clinic and Missy was the second patient of the day that I had the unfortunate duty to inform of a new diagnosis. She had diabetes. The news of a new diagnosis never gets easier to share. If anything, it gets more frustrating due to lack of resources in our disorganized health care system.

After a few more minutes, I handed Missy another tissue and offered to leave the room to give her some space. "I'll be right back. We need to talk about a few other things, but I want to give you a few moments to process this."

"No," she replied. "Please don't leave me. I just can't be alone now. I never told you, but my mother died from diabetes."

"Oh," I sat back down. We had not talked about her family history. Huge miss on my part. I mentally kicked myself.

She nodded.

"And do you have a good relationship with your father?" A failed attempt at me trying to back pedal and get all the family history now.

"He's fine, when he wants to be in touch," she wiped her nose and sniffled. "I think he's got some kind of mental condition. He lives in Massachusetts. I don't see him much."

"This is difficult news, I know. Diabetes also runs in my family. I grew up with a front row seat to it. Why don't we start talking about your social support system?"

"I have a few good friends," she snickered. "Well, maybe one. The other one likes to talk behind everyone's back and I know she has said some nasty things about me."

"One is a very good place to start."

"Yeah, she helps me with the kids sometimes. She has a young daughter too and our kids like to play together. We met at a library program when my youngest was a baby."

"It is important for you to have good friendships. Toxic relationships are no good for your mental well-being and right now I would like for you to focus on relationships that will build you up, not tear you down."

"You know," Missy looked me in the eyes, "I thought you were just going to start lecturing me on the food I eat.

You seem to really care about me."

I giggled uncomfortably. "The lecturing comes later."

She laughed.

"That's the best noise I have heard all day," I paused and smiled. "Now tell me about your job."

"I work in a factory. Four ten-hour days with some mandatory overtime."

I raised my left eyebrow.

"Yes, they can do that. And it's ok. I need the money."

"What does your lunch time look like?"

"If I can bring lunch, it's usually a sandwich, chips, and a soda. Once a month the boss gets us all pizza to celebrate the birthdays of the month. Otherwise, I just grab something from the vending machine. Ever since I stopped smoking, I crave the crunch from chips or crackers, I don't know why."

"That crunch can be fulfilling. I don't understand the psychology behind it, but you are right. How do you feel about carrots?"

She smiled but didn't respond.

"Celery?" I smiled back.

"You are funny, you know. I get what you are trying to do. I like carrots. I guess I never thought about that before."

"What kind of soda do you like?"

"Diet Coke. My dad always had Diet Coke in the house when I was growing up. Even though we are not close now, somehow having that once a day comforts me."

"Now you are speaking my language." I laughed. "My dad is the same way with that soda."

"So, you're not going to yell at me about the it?"

"No," I smiled. "Tell me about your sandwich."

"My favorite is peanut butter and jelly, but the guys at the shop tease me when I bring that in, so I try to make something more sophisticated. I recently started bringing ham and cheese with mayonnaise."

"The older I get the more I realize that some guys will act like teenagers for the rest of their lives. I'm sorry they are busting your balls over your sandwich. Peanut butter and jelly is good in the sense of protein but the jelly can have a lot of sugar. Ham and cheese have protein too, but I get concerned with processed foods. They have more chemicals in them that our bodies cannot digest well. These chemicals can cause more inflammation in our bodies which can then prevent weight loss."

"This is where it gets confusing for me."

"I understand. And I don't want you to be overwhelmed. I am your helper in navigating this. You are not alone. Rome wasn't built in a day. It's the small daily changes that add up."

Missy looked down at her hands for a moment then up at me. "I have some chicken and salsa in the crockpot for dinner tonight. What do you think about that? "

"I think that sounds like an excellent source of protein. Lunches and dinners do not need to be complicated to be healthy. Dedicate half your plate to vegetables, a quarter to protein and then leave a quarter for carbohydrates – like rice or mashed potatoes."

"I can still eat rice?" Missy's big brown eyes glimmered.

"Yes, in moderation. I tell you what. Let's plan to meet next week. Do you think you could bring in a list of things you and the kids like to eat, and we can go over how to include them in a healthy meal plan?"

"You're interested in what my kids like to eat too?"

"Making one dinner is easier than making two. It's a family affair."

"Yes, I'd like that. Thank you."

Missy left the room after giving me a quick hug. She walked down the hallway with confidence in her step. Armed with new tools, she was ready for her battle and primed for success. Not only Missy, but her children as well, will benefit from all the healthier choices she is empowered to make.

"If you fail to plan you plain to fail."
~ Benjamin Franklin

Excess weight on the body crushes the mind and spirit. As Christians, we are taught that the body is a temple for God. It is our ethical responsibility to care for it as if God is residing in it. This is both a terrifying and yet amazing reality.

Amazing because God loves us so much that He gives us the Holy Spirit to dwell in us. This gift, this precious gift, is given when we believe that Jesus died for our sins and is Lord and Savior. God cares about our health and wellness.

You may be rolling your eyes now because you have heard that many times and do not give it much of a second thought. You may think, *"Yeah, he died but he knew he was going to be resurrected in three days and be alright."* Yes, I have thought that myself.

For a moment though, imagine being tortured to death and knowing all you had to do is say a word and it would end. Then imagine loving someone so much that you refused to let the agony stop. Jesus was fully human when he was crucified. He felt pain just like you and I feel pain. And He was tortured for you. He was tortured for me. The gift of the Holy Spirit did not come without cost. It is free because it was paid for by Jesus' sacrifice. That makes it amazing, and it is also terrifying when considering the implications of this sacred responsibility.

> *Be alert and of sober mind.*
> *Your enemy the devil prowls around like a roaring lion waiting for someone to devour.*
> ~ 1 Peter 5:8 (NIV)

Food is not the enemy. It has become the scapegoat for many issues. We make choices, do the best we can and pray, not necessarily in that order. We show grace to others by helping them care for their temples and show grace to ourselves by carrying out our ethical responsibilities. Discipline is required to balance a sweet tooth and health, self-interest, and wisdom.

I am tempted to reach for quick fixes when I crave physical and spiritual nourishment. A bag of chips and a sexy thriller may fill me up and give me an adrenaline rush. But it leaves me empty of vital nutrients for my body and throws my nerves into an unnecessary fight or flight. And with my history, I know that my cortisol (part of the stress system) has been elevated enough already for two lifetimes.

Our bodies produce, organize, and manage hundreds

of chemicals. In reality, we are all walking chemistry projects. Dopamine and endorphins are both hormones and neurotransmitters, like serotonin that I mentioned before, which make their role in the human mind significant. Dopamine helps with motivation, reward, and pleasure. Endorphins are released as natural pain relievers. Serotonin directly affects our mood and there is more serotonin produced in our guts than in our brains. This is why during times of bliss we usually eat more than in times of sorrow. However, some people crave carbs in stress and those foods will elevate serotonin levels.

What starts off as a thought can result in a response full of more passion than logic. A prime example of this is when a person enmeshes themselves in hostility and becomes hostile towards others. Logic leaves the brain when feelings take over.

Participating in my favorite hobby (ballroom dancing, if you are curious) my dopamine is boosted. When I laugh, endorphins are released into my body. Laughter is truly the best medicine. Taking a walk on a sunny day floods my body with serotonin.

To thrive in life is to use all the gifts from God – human chemistry, good food, God-given talent, and the Holy Spirit – to make the most of each day. Seeking quality food and entertainment is not selfish. It is essential when we desire to flourish.

> *For God has not given us a spirit of fear,*
> *but one of power, love, and sound judgement.*
> ~ 2 Timothy 1:7 (CSB)

Kindling Courage

1. Society, in general, would have us believe that our bodies are playgrounds instead of temples. How do you think your life would have to change if you really believed your body is a temple of God?
2. How have you experienced thoughts impacting your body?
3. What is one activity that you can do to naturally boost your dopamine?

Chapter 10

Pain, Fortitude & the Gospel

The third decade of my life was plagued by chronic pain. My primary care doctor ordered blood work which pointed to low white blood cells. The oncologist sent me for more laboratory work which indicated a possible autoimmune disease. After ruling out cancer, he sent me to a rheumatologist who did more blood work which turned out to be negative. He suggested that the pain was a result of the car accident and that I wasn't "put back together properly." The neurologist treated me like a drug seeking patient. I visited chiropractors, massage therapists, and participated in several acupuncture treatments. Fifteen years later I would be diagnosed with celiac disease.

I became angry. I worked long hours, felt underappreciated, and often misunderstood. I studied and sacrificed so much of my time for my education and career as a family nurse practitioner only to be mistreated by patients and colleagues, miserable and in pain. I cried out to God at night to take my pain away only to fall asleep and wake up in pain again. The frustrations of limited mobility due to discomfort wore on my nerves.

My days were spent arguing with insurance

companies, dodging unwanted advances, handling angry phone calls from patients, picking up the slack for others with a different work ethic, calming upset people, and listening to corporate discuss "important" issues like patient numbers and "proper coding." The ride home from work was not long enough to recharge my spirit.

I changed jobs in hopes of having more time for my family and myself, but each one kept me working late hours in the office and at home. The fantasy of a better work-life balance was constantly out of reach. Guilt plagued me.

I consumed a high carbohydrate, high caffeinated diet. Exercise was not in my vocabulary. My Peloton became an excellent clothes hanger. I functioned in pure survival mode. Weight fluctuations and the temptation to start purging again plagued me.

In my attempt to help a relative, I allowed them to move into my home for what I believed would be a seamless, temporary time. Household responsibilities were agreed upon and the transition was wrapped up with the proverbial neat bow.

The wrapping quickly frayed. All things were not shiny and bright. Promises were broken. The truth was ugly and painful, physically and mentally.

The details of that time in my life are not important.

The depth of confusion, anxiety, pain, and stress left my energy depleted with little capacity for anything else. Life moved around me, not in me, and I questioned my belief in God.

The medical community did not help me. Working in the system, I witnessed its chaos. Decades of insurance companies tightening their grips on medicine have resulted in corrupt policies forcing medical providers to leave the medical decision making up to someone who has not even set eyes on the patient or obtained proper medical education. The art of medicine has been abandoned, in large parts, due to political schemes and greed.

We are hard pressed on every side but not crushed; perplexed, but not in despair; persecuted but not abandoned; struck down but not destroyed.
~ 2 Corinthians 4:8-9 (NIV)

Anxiety and depression, umbrella terms for many negative feelings, affect each of us differently and at different times in life. Our minds have a tipping point. Mine revealed itself with pain. Psychosomatic pain is a phenomenon that is highly correlated with mental stress, past trauma, depression, and anxiety. Unfortunately, we don't have any good statistics on this affliction due to issues with identifying and reporting.

By the age of 40, I felt decrepit. Anger towards my circumstances filled my body with a desire to fight. I was tired of being in pain and I was tired of being depressed. A decade of confusion and chaos overshadowed my life. I dutifully performed my tasks as an employee, wife, and mother but took no time for myself, friends, or hobbies. My resolve continued to waiver, my body struggled, and I was on the brink of a nervous breakdown. I felt like I was chasing the impossible … I failed to see that God was chasing me.

My job was not fulfilling; the toxic environment closed in around me. Questions loomed in my head: *Do people ever feel fulfilled in their jobs? Was I seeking something I could achieve? Was the pain ever going to stop? What had I done to deserve this?*

One day while scrolling through my email I found an invitation to participate in a 5K race to benefit a foundation that was set up after a friend's nephew had died. The foundation's website listed his character traits and community involvement. He was in his early 20s when he passed away. I stared at my computer monitor in awe of all this young person had accomplished in his short life.

In the far recess of my brain I heard, *run*.

I thought back to the last race I participated in at the age of fourteen! I had tripped over the hurdles, dropped the baton, and placed last in the 800-meter dash. I looked up the length of a 5K and my heart fell into my stomach. The race was three months away. Two days after my 41st birthday.

Run.

> Hope has two beautiful daughters;
> their names are Anger and Courage.
> Anger at the way things are, and
> Courage to see that they do not remain as they are.
> ~ Augustine of Hippo

Before I realized what I was doing, I was typing my credit card information into the website and ordering my tee shirt for the run. The stirring in my soul filled me with a peace that didn't make sense. My wavering faith jolted. If God pulled me from the clenches of death, He would surely pull me through this race.

After convincing my family that I was not delirious or indeed losing my mind, I dug out my old sneakers and brushed the cobwebs off my gym shorts. My hands trembled nervously on the steering wheel as I drove to the high school track to start training.

What if someone saw me?

I reminded myself that I did not generally care what other people think, and I would not let that thought become an excuse. With no one to fight but myself, I walked from the parking lot to the track, said a prayer, and ran.

Michael W. Smith's popular song of the day became my anthem while I trained. "This is How I Fight my Battles." It's a simple yet catchy tune. The more I trained, the less pain I experienced. My endorphins did their job well.

The day of the race, Mr. Smith's song started on my iPod just as we all started running. The months of training and caring better for my body allowed me to get a better time than I ever had in high school. And I finally experienced the runner's high. It was better than any drug.

> *"... for my power is made perfect in weakness."*
> ~ 2 Corinthians 12:9 (NIV)

C.S. Lewis' insights into the importance of virtues require another look by our generation if we are to become a nation to be respected and thriving. Mr. Lewis describes seven virtues in total, grouping them as either Christian (theological) virtues or those crucial for morality (cardinal). The term Christian is due to the Scripture found in 1 Corinthians chapter 13. The term cardinal is based on the Latin word that is interpreted as "pivotal."

Faith, hope, and love are expounded upon by the apostle Paul in his Biblical writings. The passage from 1 Corinthians is read at many weddings, ending with the affirmation that the "greatest gift is love." This broad quality combines intellect and emotion. We may not always feel love for someone, yet our intellect knows that we do and this guides our behaviors. Feelings are fleeting and fickle. Faith is belief in things unseen and hope is the vessel of faith. The struggle to continue with faith and hope during difficult times is a harsh reality. Friends, family, clergy, and licensed mental health providers may help with this. At the very least, we must build ourselves a type of war room that we can enter on bended knees and open hearts, praying to a God who loves us and knows us.

Fortitude, prudence, temperance, and justice are the virtues of the moral (cardinal) foundation. Prudence, an uncommon term in our day, is at its simplest, the opposite of ignorance. In my undergraduate nursing studies, the nuns drilled this into our minds as the standard of care is that of a prudent nurse. C.S. Lewis describes prudence as "practical common sense." This definition gives me pause as what is considered as common sense may change from one person to another when culture encourages a 'live your truth' attitude.

Temperance earned a bad reputation during the Prohibition Era in the United States birthed in the 1920s. When extremes of behavior are thought to be under the regulation of laws the backlash is generational. Hearts are not changed by laws. The opposite occurs. Excess laws and regulations create a society finding fulfillment in breaking the law or 'getting away' with committing crimes while wearing the proverbial badge of entitlement. And with more regulations by any government, we lose more freedom.

Hearts are changed by the Gospel truth. Not the prosperity gospel, not the hellfire and brimstone gospel, and not by the extra religious rules or doctrines. When the blind eye or deaf ear are penetrated by the Gospel truths found in the New Testament books of Matthew, Mark, Luke, and John, change occurs. I promise you that.

Fortitude has become an uncommon theme. To endure pain or adversity with courage takes a strength of character that we see in movies like *Hacksaw Ridge*, *Remember the Titans*, and *Hidden Figures*. Fear arises when we experience pain (will it last forever?) or adversity (it's not fair). Fighting fear can produce an anger that fuels courage to change the world. Even when we only think we are making a change in our own world, the domino effect cannot be underestimated.

The Cambridge Dictionary defines justice as "the condition of being morally correct or fair" (dictionary.cambridge.org/us/dictionary/English/justice). The people of the United States have witnessed and experienced an increase in legalism with a sharp decrease in justice and liberty.

Law and order are key to a thriving society. The value of order cannot survive without temperance. A properly functioning society, like the body, requires balance. We must observe behaviors with prudence. Not to pass judgement on another but to determine what is ultimately safe and wise. A close look at history provides guidance in such matters. Researching issues provides the best understanding; true research involves more than scrolling our social media feeds.

The rhythms of wellness embrace prudence, temperance, fortitude, and justice while marching toward positive goals for you and me. Work hard, be consistent, adapt when needed and keenly observe your environment. When those around us change the rules of the game, it may be the time to change course. Integrity matters.

When getting out of bed appears to be an insurmountable task, we gather our will and push ourselves out. We make our beds because that is the easiest way to make our rooms look clean. Neatness is a haven for the weary soul. We brush our teeth because proper hygiene rids our bodies of inflammation that can lead to chronic illness and dental pain. We brush our hair and change out of our pajamas showing we have respect for ourselves and for others.

I may have a good cry in the shower but then I dry myself off and put on clean clothes. My tears of distress, discouragement, grief, or despair that wash down the drain have their own cleansing effect. Crying relieves the soul of its burden, and although we may still be sad, the soul will have space for thoughtful peace.

Louie Smith, whom I met through a NeoLife event, remarked most poignantly on the ten doctors we all need. "Dr. Sleep, Dr. Exercise, Dr. Fun, Dr. Relax, Dr. Detox, Dr. Food, Dr. Sunshine, Dr. Spiritual, Dr. Air, and Dr. Water." When we pay attention to these kinds of doctors, we will present with strength in the storms of life.

Guard your heart above all else, for it is the source of life.
~ Proverbs 4:23 (CSB)

Kindling Courage

1. Of the four cardinal virtues mentioned in the chapter which one do you value most? Why?
2. What one step can you take to motivate yourself to get out of bed?
3. The author suggests that a clean and tidy environment calms the soul. Do you agree or disagree? Why?

Chapter 11

Thoughts, Tightropes & Transformation

It was a very busy day in the emergency room. Our crisis unit was completely full of patients which necessitated a separate unit to be opened to accommodate the influx of people. I had completed my rounds and sat down to chart when I was alerted about a patient in the additional unit who was in distress.

When I approached her bedside, the nurse's aide was monitoring her blood pressure and pulse. The monitor noted significant elevation in both. The patient was breathing fast and moaning loudly, her eyes fluttering. The medical evaluation done at admission ruled out any concern of intoxication or ingestion of foreign substance.

I spoke to her softly, called her by name, and told her my name. She opened her eyes and looked terrified. I reassured her again that I was there to help her. She closed her eyes and continued to moan and breathe rapidly. I encouraged her to take a few slow deep breaths. She said she could not.

"Yes, you can," I reassured her.

"They are everywhere." She whispered in between moans.

"Do you want them to go?"

"Yes."

"Tell them to go."

"Go."

"Say it again."

"Go."

I reassured the patient that she was safe, and nothing was going to hurt her. I encouraged her to repeat the word "go" until they were gone. Within a few minutes her breathing returned to normal and both her pulse and blood pressure normalized.

The nurse's aide helped me straighten up her bed and we both spoke encouraging words to the patient. She opened her eyes. This time they were bright and peaceful. She settled herself up in bed and told me she was thirsty. The nurse's aide walked away to get her refreshments as I stayed to talk more with her.

I do not know what happened that day. I have a few ideas about what 'they' meant but I am not completely certain. That is not what matters. The important lesson I learned that day is the power of the mind. The brain is only one component of the mind. It does not matter how we categorize ourselves on the theological spectrum. We are all born with a spiritual side in our minds. It is our choice whether to use it or not. And like most things in life, it can be used for good or harm.

> *We demolish arguments and every pretension that sets itself up against the knowledge of God, and we take captive every thought to make it obedient to Christ.*
> ~ 2 Corinthians 10:5 (NIV)

To walk a tightrope is a daring human exercise. Without any external protection to safeguard transport from one area to another, the human body balances on fibers or wire that have been strung together. To increase excitement some acrobats will carry a pole or juggle during their show. It takes epic focus, energy, and commitment to balance high in the air.

Most people I know would never consider walking a tightrope over a volcano. Yet that is exactly what we do when we are careless with our thoughts. I mentioned my active imagination before and let me tell you I have been down some scary roads in my mind alone.

When I have allowed small, seemingly innocent, thoughts to fester they have quickly become out of control. Think of the child who is walking through the dark convinced she was going to see a monster. The shadow of a broomstick becomes the monster she thought she would find, and she is terrified until mom turns the lights on.

Thoughts can impede our growth and success. When traumatic events are not processed properly, we are not able to truly live. They become our ball and chain that we must carry. Metaphorically, we all experience a different test of equilibrium during life. I have wasted precious time on my own balancing acts. The chaos of this world summons us to discredit the mind, body, and spirit flow.

We control our thoughts, or they control us. They are not something to gamble with in life. We must realize when our thoughts are good, keep them, and when our thoughts are bad, toss them out. To know when to run from mental environments that are harmful is key. Thoughts cannot control us if we don't let them. We possess the power to say "go."

Lack of exercise leaves a "pleasure void" that needs to be filled. Our inner brains (subconscious) want to feel good and will influence us to seek out other options to get the job done. Sex, alcohol, drugs, social media, and/or food may be sought in the chase for pleasure.

When compared with previous generations in the United States, ours is a slothful one. Walking is not the prime means of transportation, the number of children playing outside has greatly decreased, and general time spent on physical activity for the population at large is at an all-time low. When we deprive our bodies of movement, we do it at great risk. Regular physical activity, in addition to proper sleep, are beneficial tools to help our minds function the best.

Exercise is important for the body to maintain and build strength, and it helps the mind sort out all the garbage of the day. Mental stress from family, jobs, social media, and even well-meaning peers can be effectively and efficiently processed using exercise. It is a non-medicine treatment that prompts our bodies to create chemicals (serotonin, dopamine) to help us feel better. And when we feel better, we think better because our brains are not distracted by bodily ailments.

These replacements are ultimately unfulfilling. We can pursue them without regard for risk and still feel that something is missing. We were created to move on a regular basis to promote strength of mind, body, and spirit. These foundational pillars shrink with misuse.

The goal is to be healthy for our minds, bodies, and souls. It is not about striving to be skinny or shaming any of the various body types that humans are blessed to possess. We harm ourselves and our children when we celebrate extremes of weight. Truth demands honest conversations about the ill consequences regarding both anorexia and obesity. All disordered eating is harmful.

The artist Jax penned a very clever song ("Victoria's Secret") addressing the stereotype for a female body. The pressures to be thin and have hourglass proportions left me feeling extremely uncomfortable in my own body when I was young. These harmful feelings continued into my thirties. It manifested itself in a variety of ways as I struggled to push away thoughts of purging again.

The ballet class I attended when I was 19 included girls as young as 16. I could not avoid a mirror in this setting, and my gaze always fell on the skinny classmates. Looking at myself was too difficult because I knew I would never be that small.

In my 30s I returned to the ballet studio. I thought I would be free from those feelings but once again I was in a class with younger women, as young as 20, who had never had children and were very thin. I forced myself to look at myself in the mirror. It took weeks for the uncomfortable dread about my size to disappear.

Years of therapy, self-talk, determination, and grit have been key in healing my body image disorder. Never judge a book by its cover. I have trained hard and have different genetics than anyone else. My thighs have never been and will never be small. I will never be able to wear knee-highs. The bulge above my knees exists. My hands will never be delicate looking appendages. My feet, well, I will always have "Flintstone feet."

I have found that the hardest part of working out is getting on my gym clothes. I found myself without this excuse when I started wearing my gym clothes under my work clothes. Those thin comfortable work out shorts are bittersweet!! Planning is everything when we set goals.

When we outline our goals, we will achieve them more efficiently. Harvard Business published a study revealing that people who write down goals are 10 times more likely to succeed. When we have physical setbacks or limitations, we must plan around them and manage our environments, not use them as a crutch. Just keep moving.

Negative voices have been the strongest at the beginning of any change I have made. Common thoughts are, "why bother, you can't change anything," "you have too many disabilities," "you're not smart enough to figure out how to change your habits," or "your friends will not like you if you change." The lies we hear have the power to barricade us in our own mind unless we identify them and call them out. We say "go."

Stand, therefore, with truth like a belt around your waist, righteousness like armor on your chest, and your feet

sandaled with readiness for the gospel of peace. In every situation take up the shield of faith which you can extinguish all the flaming arrow of the evil one. Take the helmet of salvation and the sword of the spirit – which is the word of God.
~ Ephesians 6:14-17 (CSB)

The battle starts in our minds, and we can arm ourselves for it. We adapt to our situations and outsmart our circumstances. Adapting has nothing to do with complacency and everything to do with our inner warriors. If pain interferes with running, can we walk? When our schedules are overwhelming, can we change our wake-up time to allow for self-improvement? If we cannot make our hour work out session at the gym, can we still devote 20 minutes of activity at home? When our children are feeling left out because of our over worked schedules, can we go outside and play with them? Family activities are great bonding opportunities and an ideal time to role model the priority of health.

Another way to outsmart our circumstances is to surround ourselves with people who are also focused on healthier lifestyles. These people will build you up and remind you that you are not alone. As our partners hold us accountable, we do the same for them! Find someone who will support you to live up to your stated goals and speak truth into your life.

As iron sharpens iron, so one person sharpens another.
~ Proverbs 27:17 (NIV)

Patience is essential to learning new habits. Consistency is the path less traveled that rewards those who follow it. Do you need to run a marathon? Probably not. Will you ever run a 5K? Maybe. How about CrossFit competition? It's not for everyone. Social media posts of these events may lead to feelings of inadequacy. Remember that most posts are doctored up pictures of what other people want you to see, not what they lived through to get the post.

We are not all made to compete the same. We are all made to incorporate daily activity, make goals, and persevere. We are created to shine with the identity of Christ utilizing our God-given gifts to make informed choices and serve other with love and mercy. Adapt, achieve, and overcome.

Practice these things; be committed to them,
so that your progress may be evident to all.
~ 1 Timothy 4:15 (CSB)

Kindling Courage

1. In what ways have you been walking a tightrope with your thoughts?

2. What do you think is the significance of the armor of God? Ephesians 6:14-17.

3. Body image is a serious issue that can cause harmful thoughts and behaviors to arise. Simply knowing that we are made in the image of God is not always enough to combat this issue. If you are struggling, please talk to a trusted friend, counselor, pastor, mentor.

Chapter 12

The Phoenix Flies

The last time I saw my neurosurgeon was to obtain medical clearance to scuba dive. It had been six years since my last brain surgery. Scuba diving sounded fun, and I had an opportunity to learn from a family friend. I knew my diving was to start in the Great Lakes, but my imagination went wild with what I might find in the ocean one day. Buried treasure? Atlantis? My 14-year-old mind fantasized about the possibilities.

Dr. Phillip took me through a litany of neurological tasks and testing, questioned me about any symptoms, and checked in with my school progress. He prodded my memory, hand eye coordination, and balance. His accent was so thick that to this day I do not know everything he said but his last words were clear as a bell.

"Live life." He smiled, tapped me on the head with his hand and left the room.

I was cleared for the next adventure of my life. Confidence and exhilaration filled my soul. His permission gave me a dose of courage that I will carry with me until I die.

> *Be strong and courageous.*
> *Do not be afraid; do not be discouraged, for the Lord your God will be with you wherever you go.*
> ~ Joshua 1:9 (NIV)

In the past thirty years I have served a broad range of populations in multiple specialties while raising my children and supporting my husband's business ventures. My career began in and around the Detroit, MI area serving women's health and infectious disease patients. In the early 2000s, I moved to the east coast and worked in a university hospital until I obtained my Family Nurse Practitioner certification from Duke University. Since graduate school I have worked in private practices, ambulatory clinics, schools, emergency departments, and community health centers prior to opening my own practice.

I have consoled women after hard decisions that have implications far beyond a simple choice. I have laughed, cried, and sang with children undergoing procedures. And I have also been present in those precious last minutes, fighting for life to return. Difficult ends with more questions than answers.

I have wrestled with unanswered questions, societal chaos, and the ugly noises in my mind. And I have been the target of physical violence and verbal attacks from those I tried to help. Human behavior deserves reflection more than a hasty response. We must give more than lip service to empathy. It requires patience, asking questions, seeking context, looking for ways to help, and a genuine soul.

I have witnessed professionals who are responsible for protecting and saving lives be so enamored in the chaos of media that they toss integrity, honor, and decency aside by shouting desires for another person to die. The night that the American President Trump developed COVID-19, many on the team in the pediatric emergency room where I worked erupted in cheers and salutations for his death. All the while children and parents watched and waited to be helped. The "pick and choose" nature of the work environment shocked me, as if anyone has a right to determine which life is valuable.

We are prey to the election scandals, riots, social media rants, and unintelligent lectures that showcase the depravity of human nature. Life is messy, people are messier. We are exposed to more violence, less family stability, more negative media coverage, and less prudent examples. Gone are the days when it was considered "normal" for adults in power to save their bad behavior for behind closed doors.

We are distracted by chaos and noise. Thoughts creep in, tied with emotional nuances to make us feel like we are living life, but are we? I have allowed myself to chase down more than one rabbit hole without realizing I was not thinking for myself.

Be careful that no one takes you captive through philosophy and empty deceit based on human tradition, based on the elements of this world, rather than Christ. For the entire fullness of God's nature dwells bodily in Christ, and you have been filled by Him, who is the head over every ruler and authority.
~ Colossians 2: 8-10 (CSB)

A sabbatical to Israel initiated the pivot that changed my life. When I registered for the trip, I believed that a little historical visit sounded fun. The experience blossomed unlike anything I could have imagined. Feeling and hearing the spirits of old as I walked through Masada, the Dead Sea, Jerusalem, and Gethsemane left me wanting for more. Witnessing the beauty of the Fountain of Tears opened my eyes to issues in my life that needed closure. I had followed my neurosurgeon's instructions, partially; in the thirty-four years since that visit, life had become complicated. I was dutiful in my tasks, but I had allowed choices to be made for me in certain aspects of my life.

I wept as the plane took off from Israel back to New York. A shift in my spirit stirred me. A new season dawned, and I did not know what it meant. I did know that God was with me. I also knew that any change causes ripples; my faith assured me that all would be well.

Last year, the adult me looked back to the teenage me with awe and wonder. How was she so brave? The teenager stared back with questioning eyes.

I realized that I had lost myself in the effort to be a good mother, wife, friend, etc. I sat in my office, contemplating life and death as three of my dear friends suffered from different ailments. The roller coaster of life was on another plummet. The tentacles of grief, anxiety, anger, and resentment surrounded my mind like enemies waiting to pounce.

I reflected on my time in Israel and the wisdom that stirred in my heart on the way home. It was time I told myself the truth. I had compromised on my time, energy, and values. I allowed myself to be wrapped up in a tiny box, one that fits into the agendas and narratives of others; it is easier to swim with the current.

As women of God, I think this occurs more often than we like to admit. We can hold onto self-sacrifice as the badge of honor yet mistake compromise as sacrifice. There is a part of self-sacrifice necessary for our family—we sacrifice sleep and comfort for our babies, and we sacrifice our time to help family. But we were never called to not think for ourselves. We are responsible for bearing our own fruit, not the fruit of others. Our identity in Christ calls us to be active participants. We are called to seek out God and then act according to His wisdom.

Identifying and removing negative thoughts from our minds is not an easy task. With good counsel I was able to identify a pattern of internalizing bad advice from (likely) well-intentioned people who had (unknowingly) affirmed my thoughts. With practice, the pattern is broken. Yet I still must choose this path on a daily basis.

I actively sought to replace unhealthy ideas and patterns with sustainable healthy choices. Positive affirmations, uplifting articles, books, and music became items I sought out. My journaling life changed from detailing events to future thinking, goal-oriented issues. When I put pen to paper, alone in my thoughts, I observed if my thinking was leading towards life or destruction. In this season of my life, I needed to figure out what it meant to actually live life again.

The Gospel of Matthew records Jesus telling a particular parable in chapter 25 regarding a master who entrusts his servant with talents. This is one example of how important our God-given gifts are in His eyes. They are to be utilized and developed, not to be thrown away or buried. As Christians we have the responsibility to grow our gifts to the best of our ability, glorifying God, and planting seeds for the growth of His people.

I have observed that there are two types of gifts. One type is spiritual gifts, like faith, discernment, mercy, prophecy, or evangelism (amongst others). This type of gift is given to the Christian believer. The other type of gift is natural talent, like running, painting, dancing, writing, or math (amongst others). Natural talents may be genetic and thrive in the right environment. Even without the right environment, natural talent will spark an innate passion in your soul.

The church focuses heavily on spiritual gifting. These gifts from God are given to those who believe in Jesus Christ as Lord and Savior and are essential to building the body of church. We are called to use our spiritual gifts to encourage others in the faith in different ways. A gift of mercy may convey the compassion of God while the gift of evangelism may convey the hope promised in a relationship with Him. Gifts like teaching and leadership may fall into both categories.

Some Christian communities do not discuss natural talent at all. I believe this may be due to the fear of pride. Yet natural talent is embedded in the fabric of our being and the One who gives us our being is God. Hence, both types of gifts are given by God, and we may possess more than one gift of either type.

My passion for dance has patiently followed me around since my early 20s waiting to be released and utilized. Prior to my 20th birthday I had accumulated ten years in a studio and participated in one competition, one show, and one musical theater production, "Bye, Bye Birdie." These physical accomplishments revealed the miracle of prayer, hard work, and determination.

That day in my office during my existential questions considering life and death, the future and the past, I finally made the call that I had been wanting to make for a very long time. Taking off the lid containing this talent was a long time coming. She was bottled up too long. I reinoculated myself with my God-given talent that day by getting my toes back in the studio.

We are not meant to throw away our gifts when they look different from the gifting of another person. True joy comes from God and from utilizing the gifts He gives us.

We give glory to God, follow Him, and know that He is in control of the blessing's others receive due to our obedience.

We repair the relationship between our mind, body, and spirit when we become strong in our natural and spiritual gifts. This is a form of worshiping God. We exalt Him when we are functioning at our best, because of His blessings. We will experience suffering and pain in life, yet His blessings will keep us and sustain us.

Rest is the final key to the puzzle of holistic healing. It is essential that we find time to rest. In the Bible, the book of Exodus lists Ten Commandments given from God for His people to follow. Man has made up hundreds of other "church rules" that have been preached to follow. I only care about the original Ten. And I have enough problems following all of them.

The first four pertain to our relationship with God, the last six pertain to our relationship with others. The fourth commandment instructs us to "remember the Sabbath day and keep it holy." This highlights our need for a weekly rest. Interestingly too, no other commandment starts with the word remember. It does not require much thought for me to figure out why. In rest our cells are able to repair and restore themselves, our minds and souls are calmed, and we are able to generate enough energy for the next battle of life.

Working on my final edits for this manuscript I learned of the assassination of Charlie Kirk. I never knew him personally, yet his impact encouraged my son's faith and willingness to stand for Truth with respect and integrity. Society spins out of control and has lost its grip on reality when those in powerful positions and in Congress dare to call Mr. Kirk ignorant. What is good is good. What is bad is bad.

Orson Wells' book *1984* does not need to be our reality. It is time for those who are able to take a stand for peace, respect ourselves and our neighbors, help those in need, and spread truth, not lies. And it all starts in our minds.

Adapt, achieve, and overcome with excellence, wellness, and joy.

Live life courageously.

I thank my God every time I remember you.
~ Philippians 1:3 (NIV)

Kindling Courage

1. How can you reinoculated yourself with your God-given natural talent?
2. Have you ever done a spiritual gifting assessment? If so, what were the results and how do you use them to help others?
3. What one thing can you do today to ensure you experience a day of rest on a weekly basis?

Acknowledgements

All thanks be to God for the capacity to write this book and live this life.

To my husband, Gary. Thank you for listening to my ideas, helping with the cover design, holding my hand in the hard times, and providing support for this project.

To my children, Jacob & Ryan. Thank you for patiently listening to this mama bear, supporting each other through the challenges life has given, and for all the laughter and fun raising two young men gave to this proud mama. We don't run; we charge.

Thank you to my parents for not making me stay at boarding school for the rest of my life, supporting me through all my moods and terrible hairstyles, and for allowing me the gift of dance.

To my stepmother, Pamela Kavanaugh, thank you for your guidance and help with raising my boys, your attention to detail, and always finding a way to make me laugh. Your love for life shines in your eyes and is evident in all the things you do.

To my uncle, Dennis McIntosh, thank you for your guidance while this project was still raw and disorganized.

Your advice helped unravel the nest tremendously and make roads out of congested highways.

To Debbie Popp, thanks for both taking one and giving one for me. And thank you for all the cookie making fun, voice mail message recordings, and life advice.

To Shawn Parisi, thank you for your inspiration and for being my sounding board.

To Carol Daniels, thank you for your steady encouragement, looking out for me in Israel, and for being the perfect roommate.

To Olivia Henry, thank you for sharing your faith, fellowship, and wisdom.

To Diane Riendeau, thank you for your gentle wisdom, thoughtful conversations, and hospitality.

To my writing mentors, the late Lucinda Secrest McDowell, Tammy Gerhard, Heidi Chiavaroli, Tessa Afshar, Bob Hostetler, Cynthia Ruchti, Lori Roeleveld, Katy Lee, Rachel Britton, and Cynthia Fantasia. Thank you for your passion, delight, wisdom, late night conversations at reNEW Retreats, opportunities to serve and contribute, and networking occasions.

To Alyssa Tatro for prompting me to write my story. I finally did it, 10 years later. It was cathartic, you were right!

To Teresa Oxford for reading my rough drafts, pushing me to 'go get it done, girl,' and for cheering me on.

To the special clergy who have mentored me along the way, sharing wisdom, instruction, ideas, and a meeting of the minds: Pastor Andre Riendeau, Pastor Dave Blough, Pastor Rich Ainsworth, and Reverand Fredd Ward.

To the team at Fred Astaire Dance Studios – West Hartford and Glastonbury – thank you for your dedication, inspiration, collaboration, guidance, and discipline. A special thank you to Katerina, Serheii, Norge, Natasha, Kristina, Alex, and Ecaterina.

To my editors, Renelle Millette and Tracy Ruckman. Thank you for your guidance, organizational thoughts, tenderness, and encouragement through this project.

About the Author

Jessica A. N. Fett, also known as Angela Nichole, is an advanced practice registered nurse (APRN) who graduated from Duke University, Sigma Theta Tau.

With 30 years of experience, she has witnessed the deficiencies in the medical system and is a strong patient advocate. She has worked with all age groups in a variety of medical specialties.

She is also a mother, wife, and survivor.

She started City Time blog several years ago with the goal of sharing **C**hrist, **I**nspiration and **T**ruth with **Y**ou. She unapologetically speaks about Jesus and her faith, with mercy and discernment. Her hobbies include researching, reading, writing, walking, spending time with family, or dancing.

Visit Jessica on the web:
www.angelanicholecity.com
Subscribe on Substack:
www.substack.com/@angelanichole

Other Books by the Author

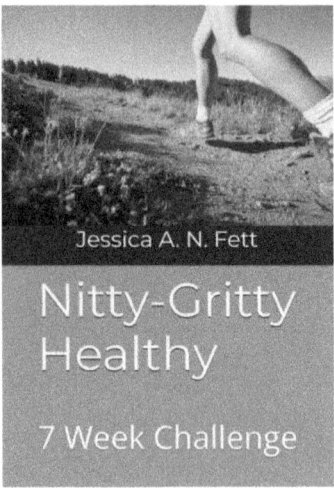

Nitty-Gritty Healthy

The Courage to Write

(Author's devotion written as Angela Nichole)

www.ingramcontent.com/pod-product-compliance
Lightning Source LLC
Chambersburg PA
CBHW050910160426
43194CB00011B/2352